HOW HUMAN BEHAVIOR INFLUENCE TOURISM CHANGE

JOHN LOK

Copyright © John Lok
All Rights Reserved.

This book has been published with all efforts taken to make the material error-free after the consent of the author. However, the author and the publisher do not assume and hereby disclaim any liability to any party for any loss, damage, or disruption caused by errors or omissions, whether such errors or omissions result from negligence, accident, or any other cause.

While every effort has been made to avoid any mistake or omission, this publication is being sold on the condition and understanding that neither the author nor the publishers or printers would be liable in any manner to any person by reason of any mistake or omission in this publication or for any action taken or omitted to be taken or advice rendered or accepted on the basis of this work. For any defect in printing or binding the publishers will be liable only to replace the defective copy by another copy of this work then available.

Contents

Foreword

Introduction

How social change influences human behavioral change ?
Why human behavior may be influenced by social change?
Our individual behavior whether can be influenced to bring
negative or positive attitude by social change? I shall
attempt to indicate cases to explain whether our individual
behavior can be influenced to changed by social
environment change. Readers can have more understand
how and why social change may influence our behavior in
possible. Behavioral economy is one useful and fun social
subject. Behavioral economists ususally research how and
why human behaviors may influence economy growth or
recession, or how and why economy environment changing
factor may influence human behavior changes.

Whether will future space tourism market
development be popular to be accepted one kind of
travelling leisure to any travelling consumers in global?
What factors can influence traveler prefer to choose space
tourism entertainment more than general Earth tourism
entertainment? How to influence future space tourism
traveler individual space travel entertainment desire to be
more stronger? How to attract travelers to feel space
tourism entertainment which is one kind of real meaning of
life travel leisure at least one time spending?

In first part,I shall apply psychology methods to
attempt to predict space tourism planner individual space
tourism desire in whole future space tourism leisure market
development.In second and third part, I shall indicate how
to apply (AI) tool to predict cruise and destination traveler

consumption behavior aspect, this part has these three research questions need to be answered? (1) What factors will raise space tourism leisure desire to space travelling planners? (2) How will raise cruise or destination tourism leisure desire and their travel desire will not be reduced by space tourism choice influence? (3) How to develop these both kinds of tourism entertainment activities in order to keep their tourism consumption balance in whole tourism entertainment industry ?

In this book, I shall follow travel psychologists and space tourism entertainment businessmen support view points to give my opinions to attempt to answer above questions. My readers will learn how to apply new space travel strategic knowledge and (AI) or traditonal tourism marketing predict methods to solve and predict future space tourism leisure as well as cruise and destination consumer behavior more accurately.

Prologue

Content of contents

(3) On space tourism leisure organization managment aspect

(5) On space objective aspect p.66-86

2.2 Space tourism leisure behavioral economic consumption model p.87-102

(1) Economic environment variable factor

(2) Space tourism leisure journey management factor

Space tourism market moral ethic risk threats p.103-120

(1) Potential accidents aspect

(2) Space tourism destinations and space tourism entertainment facilities safe arrangement challenges aspect

(3) Space tourism market competition challenge aspect

3.1 Can space tourism business bring economy benefits p.121-p.132

(1) On space resource benefit aspect

(2) On education benefit aspect

● What are the tangible social and economic benefits brought from space tourism?

Reference p.133-134

Chapter Three

Artificial Intelligent Tourism Behavioral Prediction Method

4.1 How can apply (AI) tool to predict cruise service providers bring positive emotion to their clients? p.135-155

4.2 Why does travelling market seem to similar to vehicle market which can apply (AI) learning tool to predict travelling consumer behaviors?

4.3 Why is (AI) big data gathering tool better than psychological and survey methods to predict traveler individual travel choice behavior?

4.4 Can (AI) big data gather data to predict when climate will change to influence poor travelling behaviours?

4.5 How can apply (AI) to provide travelling businesses with better-informed decisions ?

4.6 Future travel consumption behavior

4.7 How (AI) big data determine future travel behavior from past travel experience and perceptions of risk and safety for the benefits to travel consumers?

4.8 What is push and pull factors to influence any traveler who chooses where is whose preferable travelling destination ?

4.9 Why can expectation, motivation and attitude factor influence travelling behavior?

4.10 What is (AI) deep learning techniques to forecast travelling environment behavioral consumption

4.11 Environmental travel predictive consumption

4.12 What methods can predict future travel behavioral consumption ?

4.13 How to apply advanced traveler information systems (ATIS) to predict future travelling behavior?

4.14 How can online tourism sale channel influence traveling consumption of behavior?

4.15 Can apply (AI) big data gathering method predict senior age will be main travelling target?

4.16 How can apply (AI) digital channel (big data gathering method) predict travelling consumer behaviors?

4.18 (AI) tool technical innovation in cruise tourism immediate positive emotion influence to cruise travelling consumers

● How can apply (AI) tool to predict cruise service providers bring positive emotion to their clients?

● Differentiation through the characteristics of cruising route method from (AI) tool route judgement

● How to apply (AI) tool to arrange cruise route planning have close relationship to influence cruise consumer emotion?

Reference
Chapter Four
  What factors can influence travel behavioural consumption
  What an e-commerce strategy is used by internet travel websites? p.135-150
  How can apply (AI) tool to predict cruise service providers bring positive emotion to their clients?
Differentiation through the characteristi of cruising route method from (AI) tool route judgement
  How to apply (AI) tool to arrange cruise route planning have close relationship to influence cruise consumer emotion?
  Chapter Five
How social change influence human leisure need change

Human Behavioral network job brings social
economic benefits
  What does human network job mean
  Why human network job behavior may influence economy

Robots take our jobs behavioral and economy influences
  Robot job behavior brings economy influences p.151-165

Intellectual human economic behaviors
What does intellectual human economic behaviors mean ?
  The relationship between social change and human behavior

How human productive behavior may influence economic development

● New Zealand farmer individual wine productive behavior

● America high technological productive behavior

● China share market investing behavior

Why has any individual country have many people invest share behavior which can influence the country's macro consumption desire?

Can technology influence human shopping behavioral change?

Why and how human behavior may influence the country's economic growth or recession? p.166-180

CHAPTER I

Future space tourism psychology prediction strategy

● Psychology and economic environment changing both factors influence whole space tourism market leisure desire

How can psychology method predict space tourism leisure desire? I believe that it has relationship between the space tourism planner and the economic environment as well as his/her psychology as below:

Firstly, on the economic environment influence hand, it includs these both economic situations, either in the good economic environment, many people can earn high income and employers can supply many job number to provide to many people to work, then it will influence the space travelling planner has more space travelling desire. Otherwise, or in the bad economic, less people can earn high income and employers can not supply many job number to provide to many people to work, it will influence the space travelling planner has less space travelling desire.

Secondly, on these both the space travelling planner individual psychology influence hand, the space travelling planner will have these both aspects of individual psychological influence, it includes these both either positive or negative psychological influence aspectsas below:
On the positive psychological influence aspect, if the space

travelling planner has confidence to the space travelling leisure company can provide safe, comfortable, good quality of one space travelling trip arrangement, good taste food arrangement, reasonable space ticket price and every reasonable space trip for space hotel living arrangement and space garden and space farming land visiting journey arrangement, even, space swimming pool and space sport centre and space cinema leisure arrangement to let whom to stay on the planet at least one day trip, it means not one short time space trip, e.g. the spacecraft only flies about half hour or one half. It can not fly to the planet to arrive its space station destination to stay to let the space travelling planner to live at the space hotel at least one night. Then the space travelling planner will have more desire to choose to catch the space tourism leisure company's spacecraft to travel to space.

Otherwise, on the negative psychological influence aspect, if the space travelling planner lacks confidence to the space travelling leisure company can provide safe, comfortable, good quality of one space travelling trip arrangement, good taste food arrangement, reasonable space ticket price and every reasonable space trip for space hotel living arrangement and space garden and space farming land visiting journey arrangement, even, space swimming pool and space sport centre and space cinema leisure arrangement to let whom to stay on the planet at least one day trip, it means not one short time space trip, e.g. the spacecraft only flies about half hour or one half. It can not fly to the planet to arrive its space station destination to stay to let the space travelling planner to live at the space hotel at least one night. Then the space travelling planner will have less desire to choose to catch the space tourism leisure company's spacecraft to travel to space.

Hence, it seems economic environment changing factor and the space travelling planner's confidence factor to the space tourism leisure providers will influence the whole space travelling market whose space travelling consumer's space travelling leisure consumption desire to be more or less. So, any one space tourism provider can not neglect these both factors how to influence whose customer consumption desire.

● space tourism strategy

Future any space tourism leisure business needs have good business plan to outline the space tourism leisure business in these aspects , such as: different space tourism destinations of every space tourism journey, technical , financial and regulatory factors for growing space tourism leisure consumption into any one kind of unique artificial intelligent space tourism journey for identified passenger target group.

All how to design one space tourism business development plan to attempt to predict whether what trends will influence how every different kinds of identified space tourism journey in order to achieve passenger number growing aim as well as how to achieve one attractive space tourism leisure to satisfy future space tourism passenger individual space travel needs more easily.

I shall indicate what aspects to future every space tourism traveler who will consider in order to reduce the space tourism traveler personal worry to catch any pace boats to leave our Earth to fly to other planets to travel.

I recommend that any space tourism leisure organizations need to concern these aspects in their space tourism leisure business plan as below:

(1) safe space tourism journey

On first aspect concerns safe space tourism journey plan to let all space tourism travelers will considerate safe issue. They must ensure space boats that is safe to catch them to fly to planets in their space journeys. So, any space tourism leisure business will utilize previous flight rated and proven technologies to form the basis for manufacturing spacecraft vehicles, and will incorporate the latest modern avionics and flight systems for ensuring safety, reliability and economical operation in order to reduce any space tourism traveler personal worry to catch any spacecraft.

So, the space tourism safe journey plan is one very important factor to influence space tourism consumer number for them if any one of space tourism leisure business hoped they can grow the space tourism consumer number for long term. For example, the space boat flight hardware must often be maintained at the space station. It is needed to be considered by space boat experts as risky, extremely expensive and potentially sensitive. To aims to ensure spacecraft will offer an economical and safe alternative for any satellite manufacturers and other space tourism entertainment organizations have a desire or requirement for space tourism flight.

(2) reduction cost expense plan

On second aspect concerns reduction cost expense plan, any space tourism entertainment organizations need have the experience and capacity for safely launching a fully loaded , including space tourism passengers and passenger individual cargo for every spacecraft tourism journey. As a result of outsourcing the launch role to a major contractor, the space tourism pilot can concentrate on space boat crews flight training, planning space tourism passenger cargo capacity and preparing space flight manifests , and will as a result, avoid the expense of maintaining a launch operation on a daily basis.

In addition, by outsourcing the spacecraft manufacturing, it can avoid spending millions of dollar on facilities and equipment infrastructure and engineering manufacturing expertise.

(3) achieve any space tourism mission plan

On third aspect concerns how to achieve any space tourism mission. Every space tourism mission must be ensure that reliable service is provided to satisfy every space tourism passenger personal space traveler needs and let them to enjoy in their whole space tourism journey, let them to catch a big aircraft in comfortable environment of technologically sophisticated space boat, reasonable and competitive every time space tourism flight ticket price plan is developed and properly revised every time space tourism ticket price when performing their assigned every different space tourism journey mission.

Hence, the space tourism leisure company will provide one careful selected space tourism destination , e.g. Mar planet space tourism journey, Moon planet space tourism journey or no any space destination journey, it means that the space craft only needs to fly one circle around between Earth and Moon space journey etc. that are capable of meeting the requirements of travelling into Earth orbit. So, any space tourism journey must emphasize affordability, reliability, safety, customer service and responsiveness in responding to every client's space tourism journey requirements. Hence, any one of space tourism journey must have clear space journey mission and objective to satisfy any space traveler client target needs.

1.1 Methods to raise space traveler number

Future space tourism will be one kind of new travel leisure market for any new space travel leisure companies to enter this undiscovered market in the beginning. However, how to predict future 10 to 20 years , even more space traveler number that is one important issue to any new space tourism leisure companies.

I think that space tourism leisure companies need to define what kinds of space travel leisure service to be provided to space travelling passengers, however, what age group of space passengers who will be their space travelling target client. For example, their space travel leisure must provide any flight operation that takes one or more passengers beyond the altitude of 100 km and thus into space to let space travelling passengers who have fun, exciting space travelling feeling.

Anyway, for any kind of space tourism (leisure space travel) journey, space tourism leisure company needs anyone to be bring customer satisfaction, it is a plan or predictive methods to measure how to let every space travelling passenger to feel comfortable when they are catching the spacecraft (space flying product) and they can have enjoyable and fun or exciting feeling when they have need providing any space tourism journey, services meet or surpass customer expectations.

Thus, any space tourism leisure company needs to evaluate the degree of every time space tourism journey's customer satisfaction and customer satisfaction is also always evaluated in relationship to the every time ticket price of the space tourism journey. So, the space tourism leisure company will predict the next time of what the space tourism journey of passenger number is more accurate, after it has evaluated what degree of every time space tourism journey's customer satisfaction is. It aims to gather their opinions to find which aspects that they need to revise, e.g. choosing where will be the next time space tourism journey destination, how to improve spacecraft staff's service attitude and performance to serve to their space tourism passengers when they are catching the spacecraft, to evaluate whether the spacecraft can provide comfortable and safe environment to let them to catch in order to let the next time space travelling passengers can feel satisfactory and enjoyable when they are catching the space tourism leisure's spacecraft to fly to anywhere in space.

In general, the expectation of factors space passengers include the following customer value elements, such as below:

● viewing space and the Earth.

● experiencing weightlessness and being able to float freely in zero gravity.

● experiencing pre-flight astronaut training and related sensations.

● communicating from space to significant others.

● being able to discuss the adventure in an informed way.

● having astronaut like documentation and memorabilia.

These objectives need to be combined with, sometimes conflicting constraints, such as guaranteed safe return, limited training time, reasonable comfort, and minimum medical restrictions. All these above issues which will be every space travelling passenger considerate matters before they choose the space tourism leisure company to catch its spacecraft to fly to space. So, all these factors will influence the next time space passenger number. Any space tourism leisure company can not neglect how to solve these all matters before they decide when their next time space tourism journey to be achieved.

Consequently, if the space craft tourism leisure company could revise what aspects of its last space tourism journey to find what are its wrong or weakness or unattractive challenges to cause any one space travelling passenger who feels unsatisfactory. Then, it can have more effort to concentrate on improving its next space tourism journey to raise its space tourism service performance level , e.g. people, food, leisure etc. service aspects and its space tourism product quality level, e.g. proving comfortable spacecraft facilities to let space travelling passengers to catch in whole spacecraft tourism journey. Then, it will have more confidence to achieve the raising space travelling passenger number.

● What is the prediction space travelling passenger desire method ?

The prediction space travelling passenger individual desire method can be one survey investigation method. When every time spacecraft finishes space tourism journey mission, after all space tourism passengers catch the spacecraft to arrive earth from space. When they arrive earth space station destination, then the space tourism leisure company can arrange survey investigation staffs to enquire their feeling for this time space tourism journey immediately.

The survey content can include as below:

Do you feel satisfactory or unsatisfactory to which aspects of this time space tourism journey?

(1) On service aspect questions include as below:

(a) Do you feel space food taste is good?

(b) Do you enjoy this time space tourism journey

arrangement?
(c) Do you feel satisfactory to space staff
service performance?
(d) If you have unsatisfactory feeling for any one of above questions, which aspect issue cause you feel unsatisfactory to explain to let us to know in order to us to revise our service performance.

(2) On product aspect questions include as below:
(a) Do you feel comfortable when you are catching our spacecraft in whole space tourism journey?
(b) If you feel comfortable , may you explain the reasons what aspects of our spacecraft has weakness to cause you feel uncomfortable?
(c) Do you feel safe when you are catching our spacecraft in whole space tourism journey?
(d) If you feel unsafe, may you explain the reasons what aspects of our spacecraft has weakness to cause you feel unsafe?

Finally, we thank your ideas to be given to let us know how to improve our every time future space tourism journey in order to find what challenge cause our service performance and product quality which can not satisfy your needs. So, we shall improve to avoid future challenges continue occur.

Our mission is achievement of 100% satisfactory level to our every space travelling passenger individual feeling. Also, we hope that you can choose our space tourism leisure service again, when you have another time space tourism leisure desire need. However, we shall revise to improve our service performance and product quality to be better, after collecting your ideas from this time survey investigation. I think you spend time to give your ideas from this survey investigation faithfully.

So, survey investigation method will be one important idea gathering tool to help any space tourism leisure company to revise the weaknesses to raise or improve future every time space tourism journey service performance and product quality to achieve raising competitive effort in this new space tourism leisure market.

Hence, survey investigation method will be the best idea gathering method to predict how space travelling passenger emotion or desire need will change in order to achieve the objective of raising every time space tourism journey future space travelling passenger number more easily for every space tourism leisure company.

● The prediction of price factor influences space traveler number

The space tourism leisure organizations indicate the total cost of a trip into space is rapidly coming down from the initial price level of about US$600,000, it is obvious that the space travelling customer base is going to be rather small. Typical customers tend to belong to the top 1% income bracket. They also indicate that the price comes down , it is expected that new space travelling customer groups will enter the space tourism leisure market.

Typical new customers include people in other brackets with one-of-a kind incomes, such as inheritance or business sold. There are indications that those types of customers are becoming interested in spending on an once-in-a lifetime space experience. Therefore, the growth of the space tourism market is highly sensitive to customer satisfaction and how it is communicated through various media.

This will establish the status factors of space tourism and corresponding brand reputation service providers. They also suggest that any operator monitors space travelling customer satisfaction closely, as it will help developing increasingly accurate estimates of how the space tourism leisure market will develop.

Hence, it seems that every time space tourism journey price variable factor will influence the time space tourism of customer individual leisure desire and the space tourism passenger number. For example, the minimum price goal foe a variable space tourism business is currently estimate to be below US$3000-4000/kg for a round -trip depending on variable configuration and operation size. At this price, they estimate that somewhat over 1 % of the high income earners are potential customers.

However, for significant volume growth the longer term goal should be below US$2000/kg for a typical passenger, baggage and supplies. The lower price will probably open space tourism to a broader population, expanding the customer base and altering expectations. beyond this point space tourism will become into a travelling competitive leisure commodity, price competition will ensure and service providers need to rethink their space tourism marketing and branding and price strategies.

I shall also recommend how to attract the potential customers successfully. First, space operators need to pay special attention to the right level of customer services. Second, various preparatory customer operations cost, such as a travel to the launch site, space tourism destination accommodation, pre-flight training, medical check-ups and equipment my add up to between 10 to 15 % of the actual space travel cost. Thurs, solving the right balance between services offered and cost of client operation in order to earn the largest intangible benefits, such as loyalty, confidence, leisure enjoyment, comfortable space travelling journey as well as tangible benefits, such as profit, spacecraft manufacturing facilities, space stations, space hotels , space swimming pools, space gardens, space cinema etc. which are built to similar to earth building facilities to satisfy space travelers' needs.

1.2 The influential factors persuade travelers choose space tourism

Nowadays, our earth is no longer an adventurous enough place for some experienced tourists. Space tourism will be a new sector of adventure tourism, which is in the near future will be fast becoming a new tourism leisure opportunity for experiencing the unknown. Of one day, space tourism is able to reach the mass tourism phase, due to improved safety and decreased operation costs, a future space tourist will possibly only need minimal training to cope with the zero cost.

Space tourism is quite well established with visits to space attraction and launch sites, and it is a wealthy trips to the international space station for any space tourism travelers. However, if any space tourism leisure companies can attempt to find what the most influential factors are to persuade travelers feel attraction more than travelling in our earth.

It aims to let travelers to choose space travelling more than earth travelling when they feel travelling leisure need. I shall indicate what will be the most important influential factors to persuade travelers to choose space tourism more than earth tourism as below:

Firstly, I shall argue that the majority of different new space tourism journey destinations will be needed to find to satisfy different aged space travelers and different income space tourism consumers' needs. For example, the rich people have effort to consume longer time and reach any space tourism destinations where are far away from our earth of their every space tourism journey.

Otherwise, the middle income people will choose shorter space tourism journey distance from our earth and short time space tourism journey. Also, younger space tourism clients can accept more longer journey time, exciting fast speed spacecraft flying journey. Otherwise, old space tourism clients can only accept comfortable and shorter time safe space journey. So, it seems that safety, comfortable feeling, shorter time space tourism journey won't be one important influential factor to excite any young people who choose to consume space tourism leisure. Otherwise, safety, comfortable feeling, shorter time space tourism journey will be one important influential factor to excite any old people who choose to consume space tourism leisure.

Secondly, the another most important influential factor to excite space travelers to choose space tourism , it concerns whether the space travelers will feel what tourists benefits can be earned from a substantial variety of destinations choice. In general, space tourism with those of aviation, space travelers will hope space tourism will be travelling distances by air in a very short time, safely and comfortably, to bring them to arrive any space planet destinations when spacecraft reaches any space stations to stay in any space destinations.

Hence, space destination factor will bring important influential choice to any space destination journeys. As a result of the space technological tourism boom, the number of potential different space destination, choice attractions have grown with far fewer places on earth to which human do have access yet. However, the ultimate different space destinations to which many of us dream is not on earth, but as least 100 km above us, anywhere in space any planets.

If the space tourism leisure company can provide different space tourism destination choices to young or old age both space traveler target consumer groups. They will feel a real holiday when they will be able to enjoy a great image of the earth from planets. It might mean that every space tourism journey can provide different space tourism destination to let space travelers have another new travelling destinations where are far from our earth anywhere.

Hence, the different space tourism destinations will give them an unforgettable adventure. Think of how it would be to be able to check in at a " billion strategy" luxury hotel in space one planet, it means that the space planet destination can provide one luxury hotel to let space travelers to live one night or more in the space planet destination, how it would be to schedule the space traveler' vacation at one of the space tourism leisure company luxury resorts on the Moon or Mars.

This images seem from science fiction movies, but one should not forget that 100 years ago, the Wright brothers, aviation pioneers inventors and builders of the air plane, would not have imagined how, every day it is possible that future spacecraft can fly to any planets to let human have chance to stay in the space hotel one night or more.

Consequently, space destination choice and space tourism journey service performance, aviation safety, ticket price and leisure satisfactory feeling which will be important influential factors to attract future space travelers to choose space tourism leisure to replace earth tourism leisure in future one day.

    1.3 Raising space tourism leisure
consumption strategies

Although, space tourism industry is a real enjoyment and exciting travelling leisure to human. It is possible that human will choose to consume space tourism leisure to replace earth tourism leisure, if human felt that earth tourism leisure is not attractive to them to consume to go to anywhere to travel in their leisure time.

But, I believe that space tourism industry has still many factors to influence human to choose to consume space tourism leisure, even they will consider space tourism leisure consumption I is only one time space tourism in their life time. Hence, space tourism companies ought achieve this aim to persuade or attract everyone prefer to spend space tourism leisure at least one time in their life, then it can represent success. However, I think to achieve this aim, it has these challenges to influence their success, even they believe space tourism leisure business is one potential attractive travel entertainment business. These challenges include such as: expensive space tourism ticket price issue, catching spacecraft safe issue, space traveler personal body health issue, age issue, family and friend relationship influence issue, working time and holiday time arrangement issue, the space trip arrangement issue, weather issue etc. different challenges, which will have possible to influence every space tourism planner either who decide change to cancel the time space tourism plan, or forgive to choose space tourism leisure in their life forever.

Hence, how to raise space tourism leisure consumption desire will be one considerable matter for any space tourism leisure businessmen. I shall indicate my personal three aspect of strategical opinions to let them to know how to raise every space tourism planner individual space tourism leisure consumption desire to avoid every time space tourism passenger number will have decrease failure chance as below:

● (1) Strategic opinion

On the first aspect of strategic opinion, I feel that the space education tutor can teach new space knowledge to let every space traveler to learn any new space and earth knowledge during he/she is catching on the spacecraft in personal contact learning experience environment which can raise space tourism consumption desire. The reason is because the space tourism leisure traveler can raise extra space and earth learning knowledge when they can catch the spacecraft to fly and contact the space environment to learn and feel what the differences are between space and earth by himself or herself. Hence, it is very attractive to the space traveler student target group and I believe that their parents will encourage their sons or daughters to participate the time of space trip and they are more preferable to help them to buy the time space trip ticket, due to their sons and daughters can learn any space knowledge when they are studying. Moreover, every space traveler will feel surprise to learn any new space and earth knowledge from the space tutor's teaching, due to he/she is unknown that this space travel trip includes learning space and earth knowledge.

I suggest that the space tourism leisure businessmen can give learning opportunity to every travel trip space travelers to feel that this space actual environment can bring what disadvantages or advantages to influence our earth when they are catching aircraft to fly to space to travel in every space trip. The space and earth learning knowledge can include these two aspects of space learning knowledge and experience below:

On the teaching of space environment learning knowledge hand, the topics can include as below:

Firstly the space learning topic can concern how space environment influences water and hydrated minerals change , they can learn what our drinking water function how is applied to space environment. For example, in the space environment, they can learn and attempt to feel that how water can be used in protecting astronauts against harmful radiation from the sun and cosmic rays by cloaking spacecraft with a thin layer of water in the actual space environment as well as the space travelers can also feel water is same as fuel when they are catching the spacecraft, they can feel the water is heavy to transport into space when they are catching the spacecraft to fly to space during their whole space tourism journey.

Moreover, when their spacecraft reaches anyone of planets and it stays on the planet's space station, e.g. Moon space station. They can learn how to attempt to contact the hydrated minerals to learn and feel what they contained in some asteroids may be possible sources of water and fuel in the actual space environment. When they are walking in actual space environment, such as Moon planet, they can contact or touch this hydrated minerals to learn how water molecules can be extracted and separated chemically to produce hydrogen fuel knowledge in the actual space environment. This is one exciting space learning experience to the space travelling student passengers.

Secondly the space learning topic can concern how human fights space threats , even when their whole space leisure journey, the space science teacher can let the space trip student passengers to feel that they are learning new space knowledge between the space science teacher and whose space trip student passengers. Such as how to protect our earth knowledge: Teaching them to know when will be threats to our earth from space. The space science teacher can explain how this space threating environment influences our life safety and let them to feel that a mass extinction can be triggered if an asteroid 10 kilometers across hit the earth. Even being the apex species in the food chain did not space carnivorous dinosaurs from such disaster, who knows if this terrifying scene won't happen before our eyes? So, the space travelers can image and feel how the space threating environment can influence their life safety in the actual space environment as well as the space science teacher can let whose space travelers to feel and image the actual earth disaster will possible happen suddenly to let they feel afraid in the actual space environment. Also the space science teacher can teach how our earth can fright the space stones attack to let the space traveler to know, when an impactor targets an asteroid for a controlled well-times wallop. The collision will change the asteroid's momentum, deflecting it from its original orbital path which intersects with that of the earth. So, at the moment, the space travelers can image they are a larger spacecraft near an asteroid which can also change the path. Given enough time, the gravitational pull from the spacecraft will be able to steer the asteroid away from the earth. So, every space traveler will feel that they are catching the spacecraft in the safe space environment to avoid the Earth disaster from space sudden unpredictable attack.

It is more fun real space tourism knowledge learning feel to let every space traveler has chance to learn any new space science knowledge when he/she is catching the spacecraft to fly to space to travel. Hence, one successful space trip ought include trip and learning experience both contents in order to raise every the space tourism planner individual space trip consumption desire.

● (2) Strategic opinion

On the second aspect of strategic opinion, space tourism leisure companies need to let planning travelers feel that anyone of space tourism leisure is very different to general tourism leisure. In general, tourism leisure is visiting at least one night for leisure and holiday, business or other tourism purposes in Earth only. Otherwise, space tourism leisure is other kind of an unique trip leisure or entertainment method, e.g. the space traveler can catch the spacecraft to visit any planets to stay to live at the planet's space hotel at least one night, e.g. Future potential populated Moon or Mars space hotel space trip. Moreover, the space travel companies ought give chance to let them to feel what weightless feeling is in weightlessness environment when they are walking on Moon or other planets in possible. Even, they can attempt to build these entertainment facilities, instead of space hotels, such as space swimming pools, space gardens, space cinema etc. building facilities. It aims to let them to feel what the differences between Earth and space life when they are walking on the Moon, when they are swimming on the space pools, when they are living in space hotels, when they are watching movies in space cinemas, when they are seeing flowers and different species of planets and fruits. e.g. oranges, apples, bananas, and vegetable and potatoes and tomatoes in space gardens. It is very exciting and fun space trip life experience between one days to seven days. So, they believe that they must not feel these space life experience if they do not choose to participate this time space trip planning journey by the space trip company preparation.

Also, due to that the space tourism passengers need to the pre-flight checks and training before they ensure to qualify to permit to participate the space trip. So space travel companies need to concern how to take care their health check and training matter considerately. It aims to let every space traveler will feel a market segment with fitness and extreme experiences as well as he/she will become popular with a market segment passenger to the space tourism leisure company, although he/she must not guarantee to pass the space training and/or pre-flight health checks to permit to participate the space trip. However, he/she can believe that he/she is one worth space travelling passenger to the space tourism leisure company, even this time pre-flight health check or/and the short time space trip training requirements are failure. However, the space tourism leisure company must need to let all pre-flight health check and space trip training passengers to feel that it is only one space tourism which can give them and let customers view the space travel is as the ultimate showcase for health, even though a majority of the population can pass the pre-flight medical and other tests in order to raise their confidence and safety to catch the spacecraft to fly to space to travel when they are confirmed to pass these tests to permit to catch the spacecraft later.

In general, the expectations of future space passengers include the following customer value elements, such as below:

● Viewing space and the Earth.

● Experiencing weightlessness and experiencing pre-flight astronaut training and related sensations.

● Communicating from space to significant others.

● Being able to discuss the adventure in an informed way.

● Having astronaut-like documentation and memorabilia.
● Enjoying one exciting and fun space trip.

However, instead of considering these objectives need to be combined with, sometimes conflicting , constraints such as guaranteed safe, return , limited training time, reasonable comfort, and minimum medical restrictions. So, space tourism companies need to reduce every space traveler individual worries before they decide to make the time of space tourism journey. Then, it can increase their confidence to raise their space tourism consumption desire more successfully.

Consequently, instead of these consideration, a space travel operator must pay attention to the total customer experience over the entire customer process, starting from how the service is presented, proposed and sold. The service package must include training, instructions, travel to the launch site and various post. Travel activities to generate maximum customer satisfaction and brand building opportunity.

● (3) Strategic opinion

On the final aspect of strategic opinion, I think any space tourism companies space tourism companies need to consider every time space tourism ticket price and space tourism trip issues. It is important factor to influence every space traveler individual consumption desire. Due to space trip ticket price must be more expensive to compare common Earth trip travelling ticket price, so this kind of tourism leisure market target customer will be the rich and high income customer group.

On the space trip ticket challenge issue, despite that fact the total cost of a trip into space is rapidly coming down from the initial price level of about US$60,000, it is obvious that the customer base is going to be rather small and the client target customer is only high income or rich consumer group. Typical customers tend to belong to the top of the top 1% income bracket. So, ensures that space traveler number must be less than common Earth traveler number. Also, such as the space trip ticket price, it is expected that new middle rich level or middle high level income customer target group will enter the space trip leisure market, when every space trip ticket price falls down about 1% Typical new customers include people in other income brackets with one-of-a-kind incomes, such as inheritance or business sold space traveler target group. These people will be space travel new client group, when its every space trip ticket price can be reduced to close 1 to 2 % nearly. If any space tourism leisure companies expect to attract new rich and/or high income target customer group to choose any one kind of space trip journey planning to consume.

These are indications that these types of customers are becoming interested in spending on an once-in-a-lifetime space experience. Therefore, the growth of the space tourism market is highly sensitive to customer satisfaction and how it is communicated through the various media. This will establish the status –factor of space tourism, and corresponding brand reputation of service providers. The minimum price goal for a variable space tourism business is currently estimate to be below US$3-4000/kg for a round-trip depending on vehicle configuration. So, space travel leisure companies need to concern every round space trip cost, it can depend on the space vehicle number and weight issue to influence every space trip ticket price variable to achieve how much it can earn.

On space journey design factor aspect, it includes these different facilities aspects how to design, because future space travelling consumers will concern whether the space travel company can provide special entertainment to satisfy their needs. The facilities include as below:

How to design space hotels to let them to live in comfortable space environment and eat the best taste and fresh food quality when the cookers need to cook in the space hotel in the space environment? How to design space swimming pools to let them to swim in safe space environment? How to design space sport centers to let them to run more easily in one space sport warm and safe environment? How to design one space garden to let them to see different species of Earth flowers, or plants? How to design one space farming land to let them to see different species of Earth fruits, vegetables, tomatoes, potatoes etc. fresh foods growth in warm and safe space farming land environment? How to design one space cinema to let them to watch movies in one safe and warm space cinema environment? All these facilities will be any one of future space trip's' important and attractive space trip leisure facilities to influence every space traveler to choose to buy the space tourism leisure company's space trip leisure service.

Instead of these space building entertainment facilities, they also need to concern how the space vehicle entertainment tools are provided the entertainment service to satisfy their needs. When the space travelers can sit on the space vehicles to move on any planets' lands, such as Moon. A number of space vehicle options exist in the market, mainly differing based on the seat capacity as well as the in-flight experience level offered. The typical space vehicle solution is a small, relatively light weight spacecraft taking between 2 to 10 passengers. The number of passengers depends on the service level, amenities and extra offered. The trip typically lasts about 10 hours and of which about 4 hours are spent in space. The main attraction is the weightless time after in space. The main attraction is the weightless time after re-entry has started. It is a rather low-G technology and therefore the medical requirements for participants are nor very high.

Consequently, the space vehicles, space leisure building facilities, the space trip reasonable price ticket level, every safe space trip journey arrangement, clean and fresh and good taste space food arrangement, space traveler individual real learning experience etc. these factors will be the main influential factors to raise the space tourism leisure company's competitive effort and the space traveler consumer individual consumption desire to the space tourism leisure company in the future.

CHAPTER II

Space travel marketing strategy

Any space travel organization needs have good marketing strategy to prepare how to operate its space travelling leisure business in order to attract many space travelling clients to choose its space travelling service. I shall indicate these different strategies aspects whey they are needed to be concerned as below:

2.1 On concept of spacecraft design aspect

Firstly, on concept aspect, any one space travelling leisure company needs have at least one spacecraft to catch clients to fly to space to travel. So how to design the spacecraft and its quality and safety and comfortable environment spacecraft machine concept aspect issue which is one challenge to be concerned. Because many space travelling passengers ususally concern whether the spacecraft is safe, comfortable , good quality, as well as the space travelling leisure providers also need to concern whether the spacecraft is less time and energy saving efficient use, less manufactory operating cost and durable.

In general, space travelling leisure provider expects the spacecraft or spacecraft vehicle can be uesed long time. The spacecraft will be expected to utilize previous flight rated and proven technologies to from the basis for manufacturing spacecraft vehicles , and will incorporate the latest modern avionics and flight system for answering safety, reliability and economical operation.

In general, the spacecraft will be designed to carry two crew and approximately, 10,000 pounds of cargo, depending on the ultimate weight of the spacecraft. Relying on flight hardware to maintain the space station, such as Moon or Mar space station is fpr any space travelling spacecrafts to reach these space travelling destinations to stay, it is also need to consider by many space travelling experts as risky, extremely, expensive cost sensitive for any space station travelling destination design arrangement in order to future every spacecraft can fly to any planets to stay on its space station safely.

(1) Outsourcing spacecraft concept design strategy

As a result, outsourcing strategy is one good method to help them to reduce cost in order to achieve to let every space travel passenger has safe space journey experience and capacity for safely launching a fully loaded (including crew and cargo). Outsourcing strategy is the launch role to a major contracor, they can concentrate on crew flight training, planning all passnegers and cargo capacoty, and preparing flight manifests, and will as a result, avoid the expense of maintaining a launch operation on a daily basis. In addition, by outsoucing the spacecraft manufacturing, the space travelling provider can avoid spending millions of dollars on facilities and equipment infrastructure and engineering manufacturing expertise.

(2) On deciding misson aspect

Secondly, on mission aspect, any space travelling journey needs have a clear mission to be planned how to achieve in order to ensure every space travelling passenger feel satisfactory in the space travelling journey. So, every whole space travelling journey arrangement, e.g. where will be the space travelling destination, how to check every space travelling planned passengers' bodies whether who are health to catch spacecraft to fly to space to travel or how to train every space travelling planned passenger to ensure whom can permit to catch spacecraft to fly to space to travel, how to arrange every space travelling journey entertainment and facilities to let either young or old age target passenger to enjoy the space trip to feel satisfactory, how to arrange different days of every space trip.

In the last few years, Virgin Galactic has been making new's headlines with its promises to provide space travel services, and announcement that it will soom offer, at quite a hefty price, trips to sub-orbit. It is generally agreed that sub-orbit exists 100 kilometres above the earth's sea-level (Von Der Dunk, 2012). Hence, Virgin Galactic will provide travel to where customers may experience weightlessness, as well as the sight of earth's curvature. Even more interesting is that Virgin Galactic is not the only company with such a mission,there are a few more that wish to offer the same type of service. For example, some companies even aim to provide an orbital type of flight.

Orbit flight suggests that humans would venture into outer space, where they might either orbit the earth or board the international space station (hereinafter: ISS). In addition, some envision space hotels, moon visitations and mining asteroids. Although at first such statement might seem for one must point out that a "space hotel" is already in earth's orbit and that diligent progress through flight tests is almost made the commercial aspect of regular space travel a reality; it is only the question of time and readiness for the companies to make their long-awaited and open a new industry of present day economics (Klemm & Markkanen, 2011; Berry , 2012).

So, every space travelling mission is to ensure that reliable, technologically-sophisicated   competitively-priced   flight certified spacecraft are designed and properly maintained when performing their every assigned space travelling journey mission. The space traveller leisure provider will need to provide a carefully selected array of techologies that are capable of meeting the requirements of travelling into earth orbit. It will emphasize affordability, reliability, safety, customer service and responsiveness in responding to customer's space travelling requirements.

For this space tourism leisure mission example, it many include these objectives , such as below:

One trip into space, sending a space vehicle of a certain make and with a specify capacity on a space mission, provides the various grades of a core service, such as a space mission including issues such as waiting and delivery times, personal attention and advice, amenities and facilities, ensure quality assurance, it is the planned and system activities implemented in a quality system. So that quality requirements for a product or service will be fulfilled. It aims at preventing high-risk adverse events, or reducing thei impact, provides excellent customer satisfaction, it is a measure of how products and services meet the space travelling customer expectations, customer satisfaction is also always evaluated in relationship of every space travelling ticket price of the space travelling entertainment service and spacecraft product comfortable environment feeling and good leisure arrangement for every space travelling leisure journey.

(3) On space tourism leisure organization managment aspect

Thirdly, on space tourism leisure organization management aspect, it is also important to influence efficient and excellent space service performance to be provided to satisfy every space travel organization management team needs to be consists of experienced professionals who have successfully management and operated companies specializing in the aerospace industry for a number of years.

Their knowledge and contacts within the space industry will prove invaluable in assisting the space tourism leisure provider in the achievement of its goals and objectives. In individuals on the team components that up a spacecraft tourism development organization, and have unique experience in the design, construction, operations and maintenance of the major functions will developing spacecraft for launching into orbit. Every spacecraft will be built and maintained utilizing the same high standards of quality, within budget and well within time constraints.

Hence, every space tourism provider needs have one excellent management leaders to manage every space tourism service staffs to serve passengers in order to achieve excellent service performance to let them every one to feel satisfactory, during their every space tourism journey (trip).

(4) On target audience prediction aspect

On target audience prediction aspect, every space trip needs have identifies target travelling passenger in order to concentrate to choose the most popular and satisfactory space travelling journey for their identified needs.

For primary audiences example, it can include space enthusiasts and educational families both. Space enthusiasts target are usually young people and they are only 20% over 65 age old people target space ethusiasts who will be the future potential space tourism target consumers as well as the educational families target who will aspect owning educational experience for children , who is the explicit reason to visit space, either he/she has interest in history of space exploration or he/she has interest in future of space exploration or he/she feels that spce trip looked like fun.

KSCVC Visots (2013) indicated that future top markets, ranked by high visitation against space enthusiasts and educational families space tourism passengers, the US cities will include: Orlando, NYC, Miami, Tampa Bay, Chicago, West plam, Philadelphia, Atlanta, Boston, Washington, DC and San Francisco cities. So, future US space travelling market will be the top one in the world.

(5) On space objective aspect

On space objective aspect, instead of any one space tourism leisure organization concerns how to achieve its mission to satisfy all space tourism passengers leisure needs. Although, it is the major missin for space tourism leisure industry. But they can not neglect what the objectives are in order to develop or achieve long term space tourism leisure missions more easily.

The objectives main open space key issues can include such as: Providing an adequate supply of land to meet the future needs of strategic opn space links, natural areas and recreational facilities on any future space tourism destinations, increasing pressure for public access to open space areas with conservation values, competing interests between adjoining land use and development on public open space and its user groups, use of public open space and recreational resources for drainage purposes, raising higher space traveller hotel residential development placing increased pressure on the demand for public open space planet land use aim and developing public open space mor intensive leisure and sport activities on any future new space tourism planet destinations.

When the space tourism leisure providers have long term objectives to attempt to solve above these any one of key issues. It will ahve a more clear objective to achieve its long term space tourism leisure business market. It's long term objectives can include such as below:

To identify existing and future active and passive recreation needs and social trends of future space tourism visitors; to provide a wide range of high quality and accessible public open space public land areas to encourage physical activity and social interaction to meet the existing and future needs of space travelling visitors; to identify existing gaps in the public open space network and develop any different kinds of space trip arrangement to satisfy the different identified target space traveller individual needs; to protect enhance and increase landcrapt values of public open space land use; to recognize the hierarchy of public open space assets; equitably distributing open space resources; access to facilities and a diverse range of opportunities to incorporate the drainage function in public open space travelling destination areas without detriment to safely, environmental, visual and recreational values.

So, these development of any space planets howo to use their lands objectives will bring long term space travelling destination beneficial advantages to raise to build the space hotels, space swimming pools, space gardens, space cinemas, space sport places to let future space travelers can stay in Mars or Moon planet destinations to enjoy these leisure facilities and they can feel which are similar to our earth leisure facilities attractively.

These space buildings are important to attract future space travellers to catch spacecraft to fly to Mars or Moon planet to travel in possible because it is fun and exciting space trip when these leisure facilities can be built on Moon or Mars to let space travellers to stay short days in either these two planets to live their space hotels. So how to build any one of these space leisure building which is another important objective for any future space tourism leisure business, instead of how to arrange any space destination trip objective. So, any space tourism leisure provider ought not neglect how to achieve these two main space tourism objectives.

However, these are key questions continually asked regarding the viability of space tourism. They concern financial, marketing and political communities. Their concerns can be best addredded in a properly, comprehensive business plan. Some questions can not be answered definitively at this time. Hoever, knowledge of the concerns and developing space businesses in any space traveling leisure planning stages and efforts to raise capital in the following questions, every spce tourism leisure business leader needs to concern this questions as below:

Can the space tourism industry into a profitable enonomic industry?

Are challenges related to financing, marketing, business methodologies or a combination of all of these facets?

Can the proponents of space tourism to be proven business tools and methodologies in their presentation of an acceptable business plan?

Can at least a cost effective, certified passenger space tourism journey to be developed for space tourism?

What effects will influence space-tourism businesses of NASA begins selling seats on the US space shuttle to civilian space tourists?

All above questions will be every new space tourism leisure businessman who needs to concern questions in order to achieve whose marketing strategy more successfully. Consequently, marketing strategy is important to be prepared in order to follow corrective steps to achieve every space tourism leisure business missions and objectives more easily.

2.2 Space tourism leisure behavioral economic consumption model

In space tourism leisure industry, due to every time space trip needs the space travelling planner to plan how much budget to consume expensive spce ticket price. So, it seems that the target customers will be rich or high income level young people or the retirement rich old people target customer group.

So, it brings this question: How to persuade these rich or high income young people or rich retirement old people to prefer to spend spce tourism leisure at least one time in their life?

It is one valuabe research question to every future space tourism leisure provider. I shall indicate the successful factors to analyze how to persuade them to accept this kind of potential space travelling leisure in behavioral economic personal consumption view point, in order to explain the cause and effect relationship between of these factors as below:

(1) Economic environment variable factor

Firstly, it is economic environment variable factor whether it can influence to space tourism leisure consumption changing. As I discuss about economic environment variable issue will influence consumption behavior changing. For space tourism leisure case, it is not now kind of essential consumption leisure product to every one. So , even the rich or high income people who will be influences to seek this kind of leisure to play, it the economic environment is improved, it will influence they have positive attitude and interest to choose this kind of leisure consumption. However, if the economic environment is worse, it will influence they have negative attitude and no interest to choose this kind of leisure consumption, due to space travel is one kind of expensive leisure consumption to every one.

Hence, in this space tourism leisure industry, it does not ensure that the rich or high income people must be persuade to choose this kind of expensive space tourism entertainment in whose holiday or retirement time. They can have the common tourism entertainment to go to different countries to travel many times in our earth. Otherwise, space tourism leisure is more expensive to compare common earth tourism leisure , it means that the rich or high income people only spend one time spacecraft catching to fly to space to travel in their life, it is more difficult to every space traveler like to catch spacecraft to fly to space to travel more than one time, due to he/she had attempted to catch spacecraft to fly to space to travel to own space travel experience, he/she will feel enough satisfactory and enjoyment in common. Hence, it is possible that future many rich or high income people only like to spend one time space tourism leisure, then they won't continue to spend this kind of tourism entertainment again in their life.

Thus, space tourism leisure providers need to arrange any special or attractive space tourism leisure to persuade these high income or rich target clients to consume, when the economic environment will change worse. The Europen space agency (ESA), defines this phenomenon between economic environment variable and space tourism client growth or falling number relationship as: " space tourism is an execution of sub-orbital flight by privately finded and/ or privately operated vehicles and the technology development driven by space tourism market."

it seems that space vehicle is one attractive travelling desire tool will be one attractive selling point to influence space tourism leisure consumer individual entertainment choice or attitude to be changed to positive leisure consumption attitude to prefer to play this kind of space tourism activities when economic environment changes to worse. Hence, when economic environment is worse, the economic wore changing factor will influence the space travelling planner individual leisure consumption desire, even it will influence the rich or high income young people or rich retirement people target customer both groups.

As (ESA, 2008) indicated space vehicle will be one kind of attractive leisure tool for spce traveler. So, I suggest that space tourism lesiure journey arrangement needs to include that such as : the space travelers can catch space vehicle to move on Moon or Mars plants land to feel what the different feeling is between during they are catching public transportation tool, such as bus or taxi during the are catching these transportation tools on earth land and during they are catching space vehicle tools on Mars or Moon planet's lands. It is so exicting and fun catching space vehicle tool experience on these both Mars or Moon planets' lands to the young and old age space travelling passengers. Because every space vehicle's speed is not very fast and it will move on Moon or Mars planets slowly. So, any aged pace travelling passengers can attempt to play this kind of space facilities leisure after they catched spacecraft to fly to these both Mars or Moon planet to stay. They can spend half hour or one hour, even more than one hour to catch the space vehicle to go to anywhere on Mars or Moon to travel. It is possible that they can find exciting and undiscovered things on these both planets.

So, catching space vehicle to go to anywhere on either these both planets journey, it will one essential part of space travelling journey during the economic environment is changed to worse. It is extra attractive space travelling leisure journey to attract space tourism consumer individual leisure desire when economic environment is worse.

Hence, from this perspective then space tourism could be understood as a section of the tourism industry mainly based on technological development, progression and its activitity being related specifically to sub orbital flights. So, if future space tourism providers expect whether the global economic environment changing will be better or worse which won't influence space tourism leisure consumption desire to be changed. The space tourism leisure providers need to persuade the space tourism planners feel space tourism would have to be treated like an already exciting part of the tourism industry. It means that space tourism leisure is one kind of tourism leisure choice to replace common earth tourism leisure consumption. When travelers feel space tourism is another tourism leisure to replace which can replace common earth tourism leisure. It will avoid the worse economic environment changing factor to reduce the rich or high income young people or rich retirement old people whose space travelling leisure consumption desire.

Consequently , the question in relation to, in what kinds of space tourism journey message do space travel providers promote behind whether space vehicle journey promotion message which is needed when economic environment will change worse. I shall be asked, as understanding the meaning in which space tourism is being marketed, communicated is seen as a factor , which can either positively contribute to future development of the tourism industry or lead into prolonging or seen stopping the space tourism industry from its progression.

(2) Space tourism leisure journey management factor

Secondly, space tourism leisure jounrey management factor, how to arrange every space tourism leisure journey which will be one important factor to influence space tourism planner individual tourism consumption desire.
In general, it can includes these several forms of space tourism leisure activities in every space lesiure trip arrangement. The following classification of space tourism include: Terrestria spce tourism (i.e. NASA visit centre, space movies, online space experience); Atmospheric space tourism (i.e. : MIG 31 flight, zero G. flights) and astro (orbita) tourism (i.e.: trips to the international space station-beyond earth orbit) (Cater 2010, Crouch et al. 2009).
Instead of US domestic space tourism market is potential, next country is Japan. First, the study is made by Collins et. al (1994, 1996) in Japan on 3030 research participants, showed that 80% of respondents under the age of 50 were willing to travel to space and out of them 20% were willing to pay year's salary for the space travel experience. Yet, it could be citicized that the Japan people age group of under 50 could be too broad, in general different generations under one groups. nest besides the willingness to go to space, the Japanese study showed respondents motivations for travelling to space, including any fun and exciting

attractive space tourism journey, e.g. interest in space walk, catching space vehicle or driving space vehicle on the either Moon or Mars planets, earth view, zeo gravity experience, livin gin space hotels one night or more, watching movies in space cinemas, swimming in space pools, visiting space gardens, running in space sport centers, catching spacecrafts to view earth or Moon or Mars planets.

Hence, it seems attractive space tourism journey can persuade another country's space travelling planners, such as Japanese attempts to satisfy whose space tourism needs. So, different kinds of attractive space trip journey arrangement will be one important factor to influence young and old age travelling consumption desire. It implies that attractive space tourism journey will be one influential factor to encourage other countries tourism consumers attempt to another kind of leaving earth tourism leisure.

So, any space tourism trip destinations and leisure facilities arrangement must need to satisfy space traveler individual leisure needs and every space trip must be more fun, exciting and comfortable and enjoyable feeling to compare general tourism journey in earth. Due to general earth tourism leisure will be space tourism leisure's competitive or replaced leisure product and service. Hence, space trip destinations and leisure facilities choice will be one important factor to influence space travelling planner's consumption desire.

Every space travelling planner will compare general earth travelling leisure's destinations and leisure facilities arrangement whether the space travelling trip arrangement , leisure facilities arrangement and food arrangement, space vehicle or spacecraf leisure comfortable influence issues which will have more satisfactory enjoyable feeling to compare general earth tourism leisure and their spending expenditure to every space trip whether is value or is not value.

Consequently, economic environment changing factor and space trip and leisure facilities arrangement factor which both will influence any space tourism planner individual consumption desire mainly. So, space tourism businessmen ought concern these two aspects of factors how and when will change to adapt any country's potential space traveler's space tourism changing taste and needs in order to follow the new space tourism changing needs easily.

Space tourism market moral ethic risk
threats

What are space tourism moral ethic risk during the space businessmen operate this businesses as well as what market threats who will encounter to face difficulties ? I shall give actul cases to explain how and why these challenges will cause to influence any new space tourism businesses development successfully.

(1) Potential accidents aspect

Firstly, space travelers will concern that public reactions to potential accidents aspect during they are catching spacecrafts to travel to space. In fact, it is moral ethic responsibility to any space tourism leisure providers to provide safe, comfortable and non accident occurrence in their whole space trip. Because once time accident will cause any one of space passenger hurt or death. So , it must be any space tourism businessmen responsibilities to concern whether they have enough confidence to ensure none any accident occurrences in every space tourism trip. Hence, in space tourism industry, government needs have public policy to threaten or prohibit any space tourism leisure providers neglect to often check and ensure any spacecraft machines or equipments are regular opeations, as well as often renew new spacecraft machines when they are old to be used. The policy is a force effort to need them to abide every space tourism leisure safe responsibility to ensure or guarantee any one of spacecraft won't have accident occurrences during it has left earth to fly to space in whole space trip journey from the beginning to the end till to the spacecraft come to earth safely.

Hence, this policy forces any space tourism leisure providers concern to put a monetary value on increased or reduced risk of death, the " value of statistical live", used to characterize when the benefit of safety regulation is worth the cost such regulation improves. So, the country government and the country's space tourism leisure providers both have responsibilities to guarantee all space tourism passengers' life safety. It must not allow any death or hurt occurrences during every space tourism trip.

Even, the country government can have legal action to publish any space tourism leisure providers, when their every space tourism trip has occurred accidents, e.g. fire accident occurrence in spacecarft or spacecrat machines are broken to be damaged and need to be repaired during the space tourism trip. It will threaten to reduce trip accident occurrence, such as this cases. The commercial space ventures may present risk to property as well, such as a fire starting on the ground by launch-related material or problems presented by space debris.

In principle, liability law can provide incentive to deter carelessness that could lead to the destruction of property, although statutory (rather than common law) assignments of liability for commercial launches are somewhat problematic.

Consequently, if the space tourism leisure provider

expected to grow space tourism passenger number in long -term time, it must need to ensure none any accidents can occur during any space trip. Otherwise, the space tourism passengers can choose another space tourism leisure provider to replace its spce tourism leisure easily.

(2) Space tourism destinations and space tourism entertainment facilities safe arrangement challenges aspect

Secondly, it is space tourism destinations and space tourism entertainment facilities safe arrangement challenges. Nowadays, commercial space travel is looking more like a real possibility than science fiction. The usual ethical issues related to the safety of the space destination choices and the space tourism entertainment facilities, e.g. space vehicles, space hotels, space swimming pools, space sport centers, space cinemas, space gardens, space farming lands. In this strange space environment and safety concerns are just the beginning as there are othe interesting questions, such as below:

What likely would be a fair process for commercializing or claiming property in any space planets? Such as Moon or mars, when any future space tourism leisure providers who need to build above these any one of space entertainment facilities on these planets to provide to their space travelling customers to play.

How to distribute and manage these any lands ownership to these future space tourism providers fairly and legally?

How likely would a separatist movement be among space settlements to want to be free and independent states?

How to ensure above future space entertainment facilities and space entertainment places are in the safe space environment to be provided to any space travelers to play in any planets, e.g. Moon or Mars etc. planets.

So, concerning how to arrange space entertainment facilities to provide to space tourism clients to play in any safe space environment issue, it will be another concerning question to every space tourism leisure providers. When they decide to choose anywhere to the space hotels, space swimming pools, space gardens, space cinemas or space farming lands or space sport centers. These space buildings will need to be built in the safe, on stable stone lands environment and none any natural distaster, such as large wind or space underground water etc. unpredictable space natural distasterr attack to these space buildings suddenly. Because it has responsibility to any space tourism leisure providers to guarantee any one of these space buildings are safe to be built in the planet's safe land environment. It aims to achieve none any accident occurrences during their space tourism clients are staying to enter these any one of space buildings to visit or play any space entertainment facilities safely, e.g. space vehicle.

So, they must need to ceck anywhere the space planet's places to be ensured safe to build any buildings. Then, they can choose the suitable locations to build space entertainment facilities or buildings more confidently.

In fact, any space entertainment facilities, e.g. space hotels, space farming lands as well as space transportation tools, e.g. spce vehicle, spacecraft , these things will be value to be concerned to any space tourism leisure providers and it is business moral ethic responsibility to every one of them, when they plan to develop their space tourism business in any planets.

(3) Space tourism market competition challenge aspect

Thirdly, any provate space tourism development leisure businesses will face market competitive challenge, such as large spacefaring countries, e.g. US, UK have possible to dominate future space tourism leisure business (government can own space tourism leisure business). They will be main actors in space were nation-states. Large spacefaring counties can build the space vehicles, that can take people and cargo into orbit and to the Moon, or Mars crafted international space law and shaped the main investments in space tourism leisure technology.

So, it is possible that the own space technological developed countries, such as US, UK, these countries governemts will have possible to operate public fund to support space tourism leisure business. It implies that private space tourism leisure businesses will face public space tourism leisure business and themselve private space tourism leisure business market competition in space tourism leisure industry.

If these two countries governments also participate this private space tourism leisure market. It will raise market threats to any private space tourism organizations.

Whether will developed countries governments participate private space tourism market? It is possible that new commercial actors began to enter the space tourism leisure industry, looking to disrupt both space launch services ans use space in new exotic ways. For example, the US government also moved its purposeful degradatoin of the global positioning system (GPS), so US government will have effort to dominate GPS global positioning system communication business also. As this GPS communication business case, future US government has possible to decide to participate space tourism leisure business also.

However, in the future, space tourism leisure industry may contribute even more the developed countries, e.g. American, England economy. Space tourism and resource recovery, e.g. mining on planet, Moons and asteroids in particular may become large parts of that space tourism industry if these countries governments participated to this space tourism industry development. Of course, their viability rests on a range of factors, including costs , future regulation, international market competivitive problems and assumption about space technological development. However, these is increasing optimism in these areas of economic production to bring human space tourism leisure enjoyment and space mining resource development benefits. But the space economy is not just about what happens in orbits or how that alters life on the ground. The growth of this economy can also contribite to new innovations across all future possible unpredictable or undiscovered technological development, instead of space tourism leisure or space mining resource exploitation development.

Consequently, any space development technological governments will have possible to bring economic benefits from either only private space tourism leisure organizations or governments and private space tourism leisure both organizations cooperate to participate to achieve space tourism misson to contribute to global economic development and create new jobs to be employed in space labor supply market.

3.1 Can space tourism business bring economy benefits

It is fact that space tourism activities have a positive and beneficial impact on eveyday life and society and this help space travelers to understand that, despite the high space ticket prices of any space tourism leisure choices. However, space tourism will bring scientific knowledge and technological knowhow and jobs to bring humn tangible or untangible both benefits. I shall indicate these benefits as below:

Although, space tourism leisure seems only leisure activities to be consumed to satisfy any space tourism individual travelling need. However, it can assign space scientists to research and attempt discovery these intangible benefits: Such as tele-communications revolution, satellite weather forecasting, mapping mineral exploration, water resource management diaster mitigation, national security or other undiscovered untangible benefits. Because every spacecraft needs to plan to fly to space, and it will reach any space planet stations, e.g. Mars, Moon planet when it visits these any one planet, the space scientists can attempt to find new undiscovered space resource , e.g. mining or finding new undiscovered satellite weather forecasting method when they can reach these planets to attempt to do space scientifical investigtion to research new space resource , or find any space stones attack to our methods to avoid earth disaster occurrence (national security mission), instead of the spacecraft catchs space passengers to visit these planets to enjoy these planets space entertainment facilities in their space trip journeys.

(1) On space resource benefit aspect

Hence, the space tourism intangible benefits include: space exploration and international cooperation is developing sophisticted space technologies by nations. For example, the images of distant stars and glaxies using Hubble telescope, research laboratory such as international space station to conduct experiments in biology, human biology, physics, Astronomy and meteorology under microgravity environment and testing of the spacecraft systems will be required for space tourism missions to the Moon and Mars.

In the future, human would be able to have unlimited and clean solar energy from space for our industries as well as heating and lighting our homes. In the near future , it would be possible to disposed-off our nuclear waste safely and unexpensively and released towards the sun using a space elevator. We many become a space tourist in earth orbit or on the Moon or Mars. We may carry and extra-terrestial mining and even introduce the development of a multi-planet economy.

(2) On education benefit aspect

Another on education benefit aspect, space tourism can let space travelers to feel actual space learning experiences, during the spacecraft is flying in the space. Their space environment learning experience can include, for example: How many spacecraft have been launched by a given country? How many phone calls are made over a satellite? How many lives could be saved by resue satellites? How they feel differences when they are living in one space hotels, they are swimming in the swimming pools, they are visiting the space garden, they are running in one space sport centers, they are visiting in one space farming land, they are sitting or driving one space vehicle on planet land, or they are catching one spacecraft.

These space learning experience will let they feel what the actual differences between space environment and earth environment. It is one humankind learning experience education service in any space planet's Moon or Mars remote areas, bringing information and tourism entertainment facilities to the masses. The space experience learning knowledge can provide data to let these space travelers to know, such as how ships can be safe at sea, monitoring the threat of pollution, how enhancing durable medical instruments for better health-care enabling hikers and skiers to be located when lost, many more. So, it seems space tourism can bring much positive benefits as no negative impact on space activitied has been found by the society , the investments are made by the nations on space activites are justified and not the waste of money.

● What are the tangible social and economic benefits brought from space tourism?

In most advanced economies space tourism or space resource exploitation industry is seen as an enabler that improves lives and helps to develop both economic and social spheres. Space industry economic can include these aspect: Application of space technology to space tourism navigation, meteorological forcasting and broadcast of on live television and internet connectivity to lesser-known applications, such as precision agriculture, transport, tracking, resource extraction and monitoring of utility networks.

Additional application exists in the disaster monitoring and relif, insurance and military applications. Thus, data coming from satellites is important to all economic sectors, making the world a better and safer place.

International space tourism experience would suggest that space travelling leisure businesses deliver value by providing a central point for academia industry , defence and foreign entities to collaborate among themselves and with government and to facilitate the flow of knowledge and capital.

How can space tourism industry maximize the socio-economic benefits? In fact, our growing use of space derived data and systems is our growing dependence on a better and safer sapce planet, e.g. Moon or Mars and to provide space tourism safe services that space travelling service that space traveler all benefit from industry in telecommunication , health, transport , banking , security and climate change monitoring.

The space tourism positive influence result is long term, the positive contribution to our quality of life is real. In other word, the world for space tourism leisure activities is changing the internationally space tourism sector is experiencing a profound revolution.

In conclusion, space tourism leisure countries with historical leadership in space tourism have been under positive as a result of a tough financial environment leading to the definition of their space travelling technology priorities. In the meantime, new space entertainment travelling leaders, such as US, UK , even China, India have ambitions in space tourism through massive investments in the development of their capabilities in space travelling leisure business aspect.

So, the future space travelling entertainment market is large, due to China and India both have many rich people and high income people, who expect to consume in space tourism leisure trip at least one time in their lifes. Consequently, worldwide space tourism entertainment industry players are rethinking their busines models and strategies as they experience discuptive innovations, competitive space tourism entertainment and new drivers impacting the spacecraft and any space entertainment facilities manufacturing on Moon or Mars planet, launch and space tourism entertainment related businesses. Thus, we can in fact in talk about a new space tourism business, in which more and more innovative applications of space tourism data are developed dependence on space tourism data in everyday life rises and increasing share of economic growth relies on the space tourism market both in terms of opportunity benefits , e.g. India and China spce tourism potential market development and any concern space tourism job creation to every countries. Hence, space tourism development can bring positive economic benefits to any countries.

Reference

Cater Iain , Carl 2010, " Steps to space: Opportunities for astro tourism development, tourism management 31 (2010); pp. 838-845; Elsevier Ltd, DOI: 10:1016/j.tourman. 2009.09.001

Collins Patric, Iwasaki Yoichi, Kanayama Hideki, Ohnuki Misuzo 1994, comercial implications of market research on space tourism. journal space technology and sciences , vol. 10 no 2, 94 Autumn, pp.3-11. copyright: Japanese rocket society; available at: www.spacefuture.com/archive/commercial-implications-of market-research-on-space- tourism.shtml.

Collins Patric, Marita M; Stockmans R. and Kobayahi S. 1996. "Demand for space tourism in America and Japan and its implications for future space activities ". sixth international space conference of Pacific basic societies; Marina del rey; California: Advantages in the Astronautica science (AAS paper no AAS 95-605) vol. 91. pp. 601-610. Available at: http://m.internationalaerospaceconsulting.org/upload/ space % 20Future%20-%20Demand% 20for%20space% 20Tourism%20in% 20America%20Japan.pdf

ESA 2008, " Richard Garriott, millionaire American space tourist. blasks off of international space station".

published in 12.11.2008. Huffington post, seen on i01.04.2015; available at: http://www.huffington.com/ 2008/10/12/richard-garriott-milliona-n-1333940.html.

Klemm, G., & Markkanen, S. (2011). IN A Papathanassis (ed.) The long Tai , tourism (pp.95-103). Weisbaden, Germany : Gabler Verlag; Springer Fachmedien Weiesbaden GmbH.

KSCVC Visitors, 2013; MRI 2013 Market by Market

Von Der Dunk , F. (2012). The integrated approach. Regulating private human spaceflight as space activity, aircraft operation, and high-risk adventure tourism. Acta Astronautica, 92(2), 199-208.

CHAPTER III

Artificial Intelligent Tourism Behavioral Prediction Method

4.1 How can apply (AI) tool to predict cruise service providers bring positive emotion to their clients?

I believe that applying (AI) big data tool to predict vehicle buyer consumption choice behavior, it is similar to predict traveler consumption choice behavior. In this chapter, I shall indicate how to apply (AI) big data gathering tool to predict vehicle buyer consumption choice behavior. Then, I shall its what its similar points to be applied to predict traveler consumption choice behavior. Nowadays, many vehicle manufacturers hope their vehicles can attract to vehicle buyers to choose to buy their vehicles. However, there are many different brands of vehicles to provide to them to choose, so the vehicle market competition is very serious.

How to judge their different kinds of vehicle price which is reasonable acceptance to attract vehicle buyers to choose to buy the brand of vehicle manufacturers' any kinds of vehicles, e.g. fast speed sport style vehicles, comfortable and slow speed common cars, for four passengers common small size or more than four passengers common large car size?

How to evaluate the vehicle prices issue is important factor to influence vehicle buyers' choices. Either if the brand of vehicle price is too high to compare other brands of similar vehicle price, it will influence many vehicle buyers choose to buy other brands' vehicles or if the brand of vehicle price is too low, it will influence vehicle buyers feel this brand's vehicle machine quality or safe driving level or manufacturing steel material or speed or not comfortable sitting etc. different factors is worse to compare to other vehicle brands' similar vehicle products.

Thus, if the brand of vehicle manufacturers can predict how to design vehicles which can attract many vehicle buyers to choose to buy whose any vehicle products. What are future vehicle buyers' favorable vehicle styles? Then, the vehicle manufacturer can concentrate on manufacturing the kind style of vehicle products to sell already. It will reduce its vehicle manufacturing investment risk.

How to apply (AI) tools to predict vehicle buyers' behavioral consumption model? Whether artificial intelligent tools can predict automotive buyers' behavioral consumption model and predict future vehicle design trend. In fact, automotive brands and dealerships are facing an increasingly competition when attempting to manually gathering the vast quantities of data required to create customer focused programs that increase retention, ultimately new sales and service automotive business.

Building a based on that client's intrinsic needs and interests to any kinds of automotive vehicles at any given time. This is especially true in the automotive industry where the time span between purchases is measured in years. Because vehicle buyers would not like often to change their old vehicle to another new one. So, their decisions to buying another new vehicle, the time is usually after one year, even longer time. Hence, it seems any vehicles won't be frequent consumption products to the owned at least one vehicle family consumers (vehicle buyers). It implies that why vehicle manufacturers ought need to spend time to predict future vehicle buyer design choice for whole year vehicle buyer number growth because they won't often change preferable vehicle design to change another new vehicle more easily.

Hence, how to predict vehicle consumers' taste or preferable which styles of vehicle choices issues is very important. If the vehicle manufacturers can not manufacture any attractive vehicles to sell easily in this year. Then, it will lose time, money in this year because it won't know when the owned least one vehicle users or non-owned any vehicle users who will decide to buy one new vehicle or change another new vehicle ensure. The different brand vehicle dealers will possible wait more than one year to attract them to buy their vehicles if their styles are not attractive to compare other brands of vehicle competitors.

However, artificial intelligence and machine learning can help any vehicle manufacturers to find solution to solve patterns in highly to solve patterns in highly complex data-sets that are beyond the capability of a human brain, and then building and automatically acting on the customer insights it generates.

Given the automotive customer need for individualized communications, this technology is positioned to become a critical component of any successful vehicle retailer's domestic or/and overseas vehicle markets. How can vehicle manufacturers and retailers use (AI) to enhance their vehicle marketing campaigns? How will (AI) affect their vehicle sale marketing strategy? What criteria would they use when selecting on (AI) solution?

Vehicle consumers today are able to quickly access different brands of vehicle information, research vehicle products and reviews, negotiate prices and compare one vehicle brand or retailer to another resulting of the brands of vehicle customers. At the same time, the rise of " big -data mining", wearable devices that track user's every move and preference and greater contextualization in advertising and social media has resulted in consumer expectations of individualized. Thus, it seems that (AI) tools can be used to gather " big-data" and then they can make human's mind to analyze how to design kinds of vehicles to satisfy vehicle buyers' needs.

As automotive vehicle marketers can apply (AI) tools to achieve messaging strategies to meet the needs of this new generation of informed vehicle consumers, using data from a variety of sources to move from a variety of sources to move from mass- messaging to more personalized messages aimed at particular vehicle buyer segments, e.g. fast speed sport vehicle buyer segment, slow speed comfortable small size or large size of buyer segment. However, when 90% of vehicle marketers believe having a single vehicle buyer view is important, only 6% have achieved it.

However, one of the main issues vehicle marketers are facing the lack of capacity to efficiently sift through and analyze the massive vehicle buyer amounts of data required to create vehicle buyer individualized vehicle customer experiences easily. This is especially difficult for automotive dealers, the long periods between purchase cycles, and the highly considered nature of the vehicle purchase means that each vehicle dealer needs to not only track a large number of potential vehicle customers for an extremely long period of time, but each of those vehicle customers will generate a huge amount of different kinds of vehicle behavioral consumption data as they research their next vehicle purchase. However, by choosing the right (AI) technological tools and programs , vehicle dealers can solve this big data gathering challenge into a major advantage.

For Forrester vehicle brand example, vehicle consumers have more power over the Forrester vehicle brand's reputation than ever before. Mayne, L. (2014) indicated that Forrester calls this new (AI) tools is the " age of the vehicle customer", a 20 year business cycle in which the most successful vehicle enterprises will reinvent themselves to systematically understand and serve increasingly powerful vehicle consumers. To win in this new age, Forrester declares companies must become vehicle customer obsessed and the only sustainable competitive advantage is knowledge and engagement with customers, such as (AI) gathering data knowledge.

Thus, the biggest challenge vehicle businesses currently face is not the collection of a large quantity of vehicle consumer data, but what to do with that data once they have it. Even at a large vehicle data research firm, the data sets are often too big for a single analyze, or even a team of analysts to sort through and draw conclusion from. However, enter artificial intelligence and machine learning , an efficient technology solution that can continuously find patterns in highly complex data sets that are way beyond the capacity of a human brain and then automatic drive action based on the customer insights is generated.

What is (AI) machine learning tool? Machine learning is a type of (AI) that learns from data and is not explicitly program. Think Amazon, face book. Machine learning serves up relevant content based on an individual vehicle purchase behavior and experiences. More simply, machine learning is a computer program that can learn relationships between data, subject those learnings to errors functions, and then learn from its errors. The program in effect, trains itself.

Lee, T. (2016) explained that "Thus, (AI) tools can learn deep a more advanced branch of machine learning inspired by how our brain's nervous function, has also been found to be especial effective in identifying patterns from data."

When this way sound is complicated from a vehicle dealer perspective, the implementation of a marketing program driven by artificial intelligence can take care of these tasks in an automatic vehicle fashion with little to no manual intervention required from the staff at time vehicle stores.

In practice at a vehicle dealership, the program will continue track vehicle customer behavior online, merging that data with any offline source (like CRM or DMS data) and then analyze this aggregated vehicle buyer data set to predict what vehicle customer may be shopping for and what information they might like to relevance from different kinds style of vehicle design photos.

4.2 Why does travelling market seem to similar to vehicle market which can apply (AI) learning tool to predict travelling consumer behaviors?

Artificial intelligence refers to complex in vehicle market and travelling entertainment market which is very seem to be applied to predict consumer behaviors.

(AI) machine learning that posses the same characteristics of human intelligence and that have all our sense, all our reason and think just like human vehicle buyer who prefer vehicle purchase choice or travelling consumer who prefer travelling package or travelling destination and airline choice. Besides, machine learning is the practice of using algorithms to collect and examine data, learn from it, and then make a determination or prediction about something in the world.

So, it can be attempted to gather data concerns that travelling consumer past travelling destination choice and air ticket price choice and different travelling package, e.g. high, middle, or low class hotel and foods supply and entertainment places choice in their past travelling journeys.

The machine is " trained" using large amounts of data and algorithms that give it the ability to learn how to automatically perform a task with increasing accuracy. Otherwise, deep learning is primarily based on artificial neural networks inspired by our understanding of the biology of human's brains.

Thus, (AI) big data can gather all these past traveler consumption behavioral choice data to make reference to analyze whether how many travelers will choose to go to the specific travelling destination in any time by the past traveler number record to different travelling destinations, then it can gather the past air ticket sale price to different destinations and past travelling package design to different destinations in order to analyze whether it is the cheap airline ticket price factor or attractive travelling package factor or attractive travelling entertainment etc. in order to predict which factor is the most potential influential factor to they choose to go to the destination to travel in different time within one year. Then, traveler agent or airline can collect these big data to judge how to design their package to attract travelers to go to anywhere to travel or what the main factor influence most of them to choose to visit the destination to travel.

For example, travel agents or airlines can apply "Deep learning" breaks down tasks in ways that enables machines to assist them to predict when travelling consumer choice will be changed and why their travelling choice will change and how their travelling choice will change with increasingly complex tasks.

So, such as why (AI) technology can be applied to predict how travelling consumer behavior changes to bring to judge whether anywhere will be many travelling consumers who will prefer to choose travelling hot destinations next year or next month.

Then, travel agents and airlines can gather overall past travelling consumer data to analyze and conclude the more accurate prediction of different travelling destinations to the number of traveler. Then, they can choose how much air ticket price is more reasonable to charge to the travelling destination or how to design the travelling package which can bring more attractive to the prediction number of different travelling destination travelers in order to achieve to raise the different travelling destination number next year.

Thus, (AI) big data machine learning can help airlines or travel agents to solve how to design any attractive travelling package challenge. A travelling package is both one of the most important and carefully considered travelling entertainment consumption the majority of travelling people will ever make in their lifetime at least one travelling time.

It is also a prediction how travelling package will be designed that tends to be fundamentally tied to a travelling person's travelling destination choice identify and travelling package view of themselves. As the same time, travelling consumers' travelling choice changing lifestyles result in changing travelling destination needs, e.g. the country's young travelers can choose to change non-extreme exciting travelling entertainment package from past extreme exciting travelling entertainment package.

Due to personal feeling factor in general. However, I believe that (AI) big data can also be attempted to predict when the country's young travelers will choose to change non-extreme exciting travelling behavior.

It is similar to automotive dealers need to remember that vehicle customers and prospects are individual human beings with risk, complex and ever-changing lives factors, these factors will influence every vehicle consumer why who feels has vehicle purchase need, and how who choose to buy the first vehicle if who decided to buy the first vehicle.

It seems that travelling agents or airlines need to remember that travelling consumers and different features or designs are very traveler beings with risk, complex and ever-travelling package attitude personal changing factors in different travel season, these factor will influence every individual traveler why who feels has travel entertainment need, and how who choose to buy different feature or design travelling package if who decide to travel.

The (AI) big data technological travelling customer behavioral prediction tool seems to be the best travelling behavioral prediction tool in the world are those that know every one of different country's traveler need. Their likes and dislikes which style of travelling package, preferences and travel destination changing tastes to travelling destination choices.

The capacity of the human brain, however, limits us from achieving these different type of travel package sales. In this competitive travelling destination choice entertainment environment, (AI) big data machine learning enables platforms to assist the air ticket and travel package sales team by tracking the travelling consumer behaviors of each travelling customer, learning and memorizing their preferences and predicting their future travelling destination choice and travelling package design needs.

Finally, I recommend that for a travel agent or airline travelling marketing platform to make their travelling customer engagement efficient and fully-functional, I should be able to: applying (AI) tools to track every travelling customer behavior across the web, connecting to a society of data sources, CRM, DMS, third-party, web travelling brands, social traveler email, click etc., aggregating and accurately cross-reference data from a variety of sources, leveraging this data to drive insights on a mass scale, as well as on an individualized basis, driving actions and automatically direct travelling customer engagement via multiple channels based on where each customer is in their travelling individual lifecycle.

4.3 Why is (AI) big data gathering tool better than psychological and survey methods to predict traveler individual travel choice behavior?

Prediction travel behavioral consumption from psychology and survey methods.

How to predict travel consumption? It is one question to any travel agents concern to use what methods which can predict how many numbers of travelers where who will choose to go to travel more accurately. I think that who can consider how to predict travel behavioral consumption from psychology and survey travel choice prediction method, but it is better to apply (AI) big data gathering method to predict travel consumer's destination choice more accurate. The reason is as below:

The first reason is that traveller individual travel psychological desire is difficult to predict accurate more than (AI) big data gathering method, it is due that the data is past traveler's destination choice and travel package and ticket price actual data from (AI) big data gathering method. Otherwise, survey investigation is only traveler psychological thinking method. It lacks enough past actual traveler data gathering.

The second reason is that on the weakness of traveler individual psychological thinking view of survey investigation. It has evidence to support the relationship between self-identify threat and resistance to change travel behavior to any travelers, controlling for whose past travelling behavior, resistance to change if a psychological phenomenon of long standing interest in many applied branches of psychology.

Past travelling behavior has been acknowledged as a predictor of future action. Such as travelling behavior that is experienced as successful is likely to be repeated and may lead to habitual patterns. Some psychologists differentiate habit between two concepts, such as goal oriented and automatic oriented both. Although repeated past travelling behavior is addition goal oriented and automatic oriented. Further non-deliberative nature of habit may make appeals to judge and to predict future individual traveler's behavior accurately.

However, repeated one traveler will choose the destination to repeat to travel without a necessary constraint of goal orientation and automatic oriented both. So, it seems that psychological factor can influence any individual traveler why and how who choose to decide to repeat to choose the destination to travel.

So, survey investigation is only the traveler's thinking to answer the travel firm. It is not sure that the traveler's past travel experience is real answer. Otherwise, (AI) big data gathering method is computer gathering method which gather past traveler consumption actual data to analyze and conclude future traveler possible repeated travel destination choice and travel package choice more accurate.

The third reason is that on the strength of (AI) big data gathering method computer statistic view to predict future traveller consumer's destination and travel package choice. It is structural equation modeling is an extremely flexible linear-in-parameters multivariate statistical modeling technique. It has been used in modeling travel behavior and values since about 1980 year. It is a software method to handle a large number of variables, as well as unobserved variables specified as linear combinations (weighted averages) of the observed variable.

4.4 Can (AI) big data gather data to predict when climate will change to influence poor travelling behaviours?

(AI) big data tool can predict the flexibility of human travelling behavioral change is at least the result of one such mechanism, our ability to travel mentally in time and entertain potential future. Understanding of the impacts is holidays, particularly those involving travel.

Using focus groups research to explores tourists' awareness of the impacts of travel own climate change, examines the extent to which climate change features in holiday travel decisions and identifies some of the barriers to the adoption of less carbon intensive tourism practices.

The findings suggest many tourists don't consider climate change when planning their holidays. The failure of tourists to engage with the climate change to impact of holidays, combined with significant barriers to behavioral change, presents a considerable challenge in the tourism industry. In the future, computer (AI) big data tool can attempt to predict when the country's climate change to influence travelers to choose to go to the country to travel, e.g. next month or next half year or next year hot travelling destinations.

Tourism is a highly energy intensive industry and has only recently attracted attention as an important contributions to climate change through greenhouse gas emissions. It has been estimated that tourism contributes 5% of global carbon dioxide emissions. There have been a number of potential changes proposed for reducing the impact of air travel on climate change. These include technological changes, market based changes and behavioral changes.

However, the role that climate change plays in the holiday and travel decisions of global tourists. How the global tourists of the impacts travel has on climate change to establish the extent to which climate change, considerations features in holiday travel decision making processes and to investigate the major barriers to global tourists adopting less carbon intensive travel practices. It will bring this question: Will tourists aware the impacts that their holidays and travel have on climate changes to influence their travelling decision?

When, it comes to understand individual traveler's behavioral change, wide range of conceptual theories have been developed, utilizing various social, psychological, subjective and objective variables in order to model travel consumption behavior. These theories of travel behavioral change operate at a number of different levels, including the individual level, the interpersonal level and community level. Whether pro-environmental behavior can be used to predict travel consumption behavior in a climate change. However, the question of what determines pro-environmental behavior in such a complex one that it can not be visualized through one single framework or diagram.

Despite the potentially high risk scenario for the tourism industry and the global environment, the tourism and climate change ought have close relationship.

However, (AI) big data tool can be applied to find what factors to influence the time of travelers' travelling choices. What are the important factors and variables which can limit tourism? e.g. money, time, family problem, extreme hot or cold weather change, air ticket price, journey attraction etc. variable factors.

Mention of holidays and travel were deliberately avoided in the recruitment process, so as not to create a connection factor to influence traveler's individual mind. However, the dismissal of alternative transportation modes can be conceived as either a structural barrier, in the sense that flying is perhaps the only realistic option to reach long-haul holiday destination, or a perceived behavioral control barriers in that an individual perceives flying as the only option open to whom.

The transportation tool factor will be depend to extent on the distance to the destination. This can also be interpreted in a social perspective as an intention with the resources available where much international tourism is structured around flying. To increase the availability of different transportation modes, tourists could choose holiday destination closer to home.

Finally, also how to predict future travel behavioral consumption. I feel that travel agents need to predict whether any country's random daily variation of weather factor is also important to influence travel behavior. e.g. in weather, temperature, rainfall and snowfall with traffic accidents factors will have relationship to cause travel demand.

Some scientists estimate suggest that when warmed temperatures and reduced snowfall are associated with a moderate decline in non-fatal accidents, they are also associated with a significant increase in fatal accidents. Thus increase in fatalities and temperature. Half of the estimated effect of temperature on fatalities is due to changes in the exposure to pedestrians, bicyclists and motorcyclists as temperature increase.

So, if any countries have rainfall, snowfall and low temperature to cause traffic accidents, whether this accident occurrence will influence the travelers who liking climb snow hills, riding bicycle, running sports who will avoid to travel to these countries' bad weather after occurs. So, why I feel that this natural climate factor will also be one serious factor to influence travel behavioral consumption. However, (AI) big data tool can predict more accurate than survey method when climate change to influence the country's climate to be poor, then it can predict when which countries are not popular acceptable to global country consumers' travel choice next month.

4.5 How can apply (AI) to provide travelling businesses with better-informed decisions ?

I shall explain how (AI) big data gathering technology can provide travelling businesses with better-informed decisions to drive top-line growth, deliver meaningful experience for travelling customers and smooth their path along the travelling consumer journey. The widely understood definition of (AI) involves the ability of machines or computers to learn human thinking, reasoning and decision-making abilities.

So, such as (AI) learning machine system can attempt to learn travelling consumer's travel destination or travel package thinking, judgement of their reasons why they choose to go to the destination to travel or why they choose to buy the travel package and learn how and why they make their past travelling decisions from their past travel big data gathering.

A Narrative science study in 2015 year identified that (AI) was being used primarily in voice recognition, machine learning virtual assistants and decision support. This study also highlighted the many branches of (AI) and that techniques and their definition are used interchangeably. It is possible that (AI) can be used to gather big data , then to analyze to help travel businesses to predict travelling consumer travel destination and travel package choice behaviors. For example, one of the most common techniques is traveler machine learning, where algorithms are used to perform tasks by learning from the airline or travel agent whose past all travelers' travelling destination choice and travel package choice historical data.

However, during 2017 year, search engines will begin to find what additional factors can influence past traveler personal travelling destination and travelling package travelling behavioral data into prediction of future travelling customer behavioral results, such as the online traveler (user's) history of travelling data searches, such as anywhere are the most popular travelling locations or travelling destinations and previously captures conservations.

Artificial intelligence will use this past travelling

destinations and travelling package information to power predictive search results, e.g. predictive future travelling consumer's choice behavioral processing for where will be their preferable travelling destination choice and how to design travelling package to satisfy future travelling clients' needs.

Predictive search will improve the quality of online travelling search results, and provide new insights into travelling consumers' travelling destination and package behavior and the moments which matter to them. Search will give recommendation into tailored how travelling consumer individual travelling destination choice in travelling decision making process. Several of the largest online platforms already use (AI) travelling machine learning to improve predictive travelling consumer behavioral search results.

For example, Google's rank brain technology adds research by understanding the context in which the travelling consumer has entered it. Over time, rank brain will learn further from user behaviors Amazon's DSSTNE (pronouned destiny) learns from shoppers' purchasing habits and consumption behavior to offer better product recommend actions, which Amazon can offer before a consumer has entered anything into the search bar.

Such as (AI) big data can gather past online travelers' e-ticket purchase transactions to conclude that online traveler's travelling choice habits and online traveler consumption behavior to offer better travelling destinations and travelling package opinions to travel agents or airlines. However, this technology is not independent of human input. For example, Google engineers will periodically retain the rank brain system to improve the models it uses.

For another example, in 2016 year , Apple computer revamped its travelling scene photos app to allow travelling consumers to search for specific travelling destinations in the travelling scene phots, they want to find anywhere travelling destination photos, not just dates and locations. Each travelling photo that an intelligent phone or intelligent pad user takes goes through 11 billion computations, so that travelling scene photos can understand exactly where is the travelling destination photography to let online travelling consumer to feel anywhere they plan to go to the location to travel. So, (AI) learning machine can make online travelling photos more attractive to influence potential travelers choose to the destination to travel after they see the travelling destination scene photos from internet.

It seems that in future, (AI) machine learning will allow online travelling search to evolve even further. Search engineers will deliver refined recommendations to airlines' online traveler e-ticket search users and use less human input to predict travelling consumers' needs from internet channel. For IBM computer example, it indicated 90% of the data that exists today has been created in the last two years.

This huge explosion of past traveler's e-ticket consumption data gives the opportunity to quickly spot and react to the latest trends, fashion and fads among its travelling clients and potential clients. This will allow airline or travel agent companies to better engage with younger travelling consumers, who gain influence access to the latest travelling destination and package trends.

They associate with to help define who they are as individuals. Thus, travelling company brands have to identify and make use of them before travelling consumers move on, but the vast quantity of past e-ticket purchase data available makes from internet channel. This a resource-intensive task. For next example, Lesara, a based online clothes store, uses this machine learning to inform its product decision often gathering information from internal and external sources.

When its trends -spotting shoes. Lesara has a range of over 20 styles and sells hundreds of pairs a day. It focus on giving consumers, the very latest trends allow Lesara to develop on average of 50,000 new items each year. It compared to 11,000 old items each year. Thus, travelling agents or airlines can attempt to apply (AI) big data gathering method to gather all past e-ticket purchase data, concerns where they prefer to choose to go to the destinations to travel and what travelling packages are the most attractive to the travelers to choose to buy. It aims to help them to predict where future travelers will prefer to choose to go to travel or what travelling package they will prefer to choose to buy next year.

For another (AI) big data prediction example, Lesara is one online clothes store, uses machine learning decisions after gathering information from internal and external sources. One of its most popular products, shoes with LED started life when its trend spotting software flagged up a blogger wearing similar shoes. Now Lesara has a range of over 20 styles and sells hundreds of pairs a day. Its focus on giving consumers the very latest trends allows Lesara to develop an average of 50,000 new items each year, compared to 11,000 for its competitor Lara.

It seems (AI) big data gathering machine learning can help Lesara business to predict what kinds of shoes design or style that shoe consumers will prefer choose to buy in future shoe market trend. Thus, Lesara can predict shoe consumers' taste successfully and it can manufacture many attractive style of shoes.

(AI) machine learning can gather global past shoe consumer's shoe shopping experiences, then analyzes to make conclusion to give lesara recommendation successfully. This will make the experience more enjoyable for shoe consumers and allow Lesara to advert whose different new style or design of shoes to deliver them move relevant messages by understanding the context of the experience.

So, online travel agents or online airline can also attempt to apply (AI) big data gathering method to predict where travelers will prefer to go to travel and how they ought design travelling packages to attract them to choose to buy next year. Hence, (AI) big data gathering technology can conclude how to design traveler agents' travelling package products to be the most attractive to excite many travelers choose to buy their travelling package, due to it has more accurate to predict travelling consumer destination and travelling package choice behaviors to compare human themselves prediction judgement effort, e.g. travelling survey or marketing research, or telephone enquire. It seems that (AI) machine judgement effort is more accurate to compare to human judgment effort in travelling industry.

4.6 Future travel consumption behavior

Can (AI) big data gathering tool predict traveler individual habitual behavior , e.g. renting travel transportation tools ?

Can (AI) big data gathering tool can predict past traveler destination and travelling package choice habit and it can be intended to predict of future traveler behavior to people are creatures of habits judgement of future anywhere travelling destination choice next year or next month or next half year destination prediction ?

Many of human's everyday goal-directed behaviors are performed in a habitual fashion, the transportation made and route one takes to work, one's choice of breakfast. Habits are formed when using the some behavior frequently and a similar consistency in a similar context for the some purpose whether the individual past travel consumption model will be caused a habit to whom. e.g. choosing whom travel agent to buy air ticket or traveling package; choosing the same or similar countries' destinations to go to travel ; choosing the business class or normal (general) class of quality airlines to catch planes.

Does habitual rent traveling car tools use not lead to more resistance to change of travel mode? It has been argued that past behavior is the best predictor of future behavior to travel consumption. If individual traveler's past consumption behavior was always reasoned, then frequency of prior travel consumption behavior should only have an indirect link to the individual traveler's behavior. It seems that renting travel car tools to use is a habit example. So, a strong rent traveling car tools useful habit makes traveling mode choice. People with a strong renting of traveling car tools of habit should have low motivation to attend to gather any information about public transportation in their choice of travelling country for individual or family or friends members during their traveling journeys.

Even when persuasive communication changes the traveler whose attitudes and intention, in the case of individual traveler or family travelers with a strong renting travel car tools habit. It is difficult to change whose travel behaviors to choose to catch public transportation in whose any trips in any countries. However, understanding of travel behavior and the reasons for choosing one mode of transportation over another. The arguments for rent traveling car tools to use, including convenience, speed, comfort and individual freedom and well known.

Increasingly, psychological factors include such as, perceptions, identity, social norms and habit are being used to understand travel mode choice. Whether how many travel consumers will choose to rent traveling car tools during their trips in any countries. It is difficult to estimate the numbers. As the average level of renting travel car tools of dependence or attitudes to certain travel package policies from travel agents. Instead different people must be treated in different ways because who are motivated in different ways and who are motivated by different travel package policies ways from travel agents.

In conclusion, the factors influence whose traveler's individual traveler destination choice behavior The factors include either who chooses to rent traveling car tools or who chooses to catch public transportation when who individual goes to travel in alone trip or family trip. It include influence mode choice factors, such as social psychology factor and marketing on segmentation factor both to influence whose transportation choice of behavior in whose trip. So, (AI) big data can be attempted to gather past traveler transportation tool choice, rent travelling car tools choice or catching public transportation tools choice to predict where destination can provide what kind of transportation tool to attract many travelers to choose to go to the place to travel.

4.7 How (AI) big data determine future travel behavior from past travel experience and perceptions of risk and safety for the benefits to travel consumers?

How (AI) big data determine future travel behavior from past travel experience and perceptions of risk and safety for the benefits to travel consumers? Why does individual traveler avoid certain destination(s) is(are) as relevant to tourist decision making as why who chooses to travel to others?

Perceptions of risk and safety and travel experience are likely to influence travel decisions. If travel agents had efforts to predict future travel behavior to guess whether travelers will feel where is(are) risk and unsafe to cause who does not choose to go to the country to travel. Then, the travel agents will avoid to choose to spend much time to design the different traveling package to attract their potential travel consumers to choose to travel. The reason is because in the case of individual traveler's tourism experience, the traveler whose past disappointment travel experience (psychological risk) will be a serious threat to the traveler's health or life (health, physical or terrorism risk). The past safety or unhealthy risk to the country(countries) will influence the traveler decides to choose not to go to the countries(country) to travel again in the future.

4.8 What is push and pull factors to influence any traveler who chooses where is whose preferable travelling destination ?

How to apply (AI) big data to predict individual traveler's behavioral intention of choosing a travel destination?

Understanding why people travel and what factors influence their behavioral intention of choosing a travel destination is beneficial to tourism planning and marketing.

In general, an individual's choice of a travel destination into two forces.

The first force is the push factor that pushes an individual away from home and attempt to develop a general desire to go somewhere, without specifying where that may be.

The other force is the pull factor that pull an individual toward in destination, due to a region-specific or perceived attractiveness of a destination. The respective push and pull factors illustrate that people travel because who are pushed by whose internal motives and pulled by external forced of a destination. However, the decision making process leading to the choice of a travel destination is a very complex process. For example, a Taiwanese traveler who might either choose new travel destination of Hong Kong or another old travel Asia destinations again or who also might choose any one of Western country, as a new travel destination. The travel agents can predict where who will have intention to choose to travel from whose past behavior and attitude, subjective and perceived behavioral control model. When (AI) big data gather past every country traveler number who chose to go to which countries to travel in order to judge where destinations will be the country travelers' travelling choice destinations in the future.

The factors influence where is the traveler choice, include personal safety, scenic beauty, cultural interest, climate changing, transportation tools, friendliness of local people, price of trip, trip package service in hotels and restaurants, quality and variety of food and shopping facilities and services etc. needs. So, whose factors will influence where is the individual travel's choice. It seems every traveler whose choice of travel process, will include past behavior. e.g. travelling experience, travelling habit, then to choose the best seasoned travelling action to satisfy whose travel needs. This process is the individual traveler's psychological choice process, who must need time to gather information to compare concerning of different travel packages, destination scene, climate change, transportation tools available to the destination, air ticket price etc. these factors, then to judge where is the best right destination to travel in the right time.

Hence, (AI) big data can gather past different countries' climate changing data, transportation tool changing data, destination scene environment changing etc. different data to give opinions to travelling businesses whether any country's these above factors will influence about how many traveler number will be increase or decrease in the future.

4.9 Why can expectation, motivation and attitude factor influence travelling behavior?

Social psychology is concerned with gaining insight into the psychological of socially relevant behaviors and the processes. For instance, on a global level bad influence to global warming, it influences some countries extreme cold or hot bad climate changing occurrence, then it ought influence some travelers' behavioral decision to change their mind to choose some countries to go to travel at the moment which do not occur extreme hot or cold climate (temperature). e.g. above than 40 degree in summer or below than 0 degree in winter. Due to the extreme climate changing environment in the countries, it will cause them to feel uncomfortable to play during their trips. So, the global warming causes to climate changing factor will influence the numbers of travel consumption to be reduced possibly. This is global climate changing environment factor influences to bad or uncomfortable social psychological feeling to global travelers' mind of traveling decision. What is individual traveler expectation, motivation and attitude? Tourism sector includes inbound (domestic) tourism and outbound (overseas) tourism both incomes to any countries. According to recent article, a tourist behavior model has been developed, called the expectation, motivation and attitude (EMA) model (Hsu et al., 2010).

This model focuses on the pre-visit stage of tourists by modeling the behavioral process by incorporating expectation, motivation and attitude. Travel motivation is considered as an essential component of the behavioral process, which has been increasing attention from the travel; industry. The economic approach defines "tourism" is an identifiable nationally important industry. It includes the component activities of transportation, accommodation, recreation, food and related service. So, tourism behavioral consumption is concerned the individual tourist's usual habituate of the industry which responds to whose needs, and of the impacts that both the tourist and the tourism industry have on the socio-cultural, economic and physical environment.

However, travel motivation means how to understand and predict factors that influence travel decision making. According to Backman and others (1995, p.15), motivation is conceptually viewed as " a state of need, a condition that services as a driving force to display different kind of behavior toward certain types of activities, developing preferences, arriving at some expected satisfactory outcome." So, motivation and expectancy which has close relationship to any tourist before who decided to do any tourism of behavior.

Some economists confirmed motivation and expectancy

which has relations, such as expectation of visiting an outbound destination has a direct effect on motivation to visit the destination; motivation has a direct effect on attitude toward visiting the destination; expectation of visiting the outbound destination has a direct affection on attitude toward visiting the destination and motivation has a mediating effect on the relationship in between expectation and attitude.

Hence, (AI) big data can gather all the country's climate environment change, transportation tool change, entertainment scene change, hotel price and restaurant price change etc. data to give opinions whether the country will attract how many traveler to choose to go to travel in the year.

4.10 What is (AI) deep learning techniques to forecast travelling environment behavioral consumption

Prediction how many travelers will choose to go to the country to travel. It is similar to apply deep-learning technology to predict how to raise the agricultural farming productivity in the agricultural export country.

The (AI) deep-learning technology leads to performance enhancement and generalization of artificial intelligent technology. It influences the global leader in the field of information technology has declared its intention to utilize the deep-learning technology to solve environmental problems, such as climate change.

So, it will help agriculture farming businesses can raise any plant food: vegetable, fruit, rice which grow up very easily if farmers can apply (AI) deep-learning technology to solve environment problems to influence their plant food grow. If the whole year seasonal change is very good and it is suitable for any plant food to grow in farming land easily, e.g. rain is enough and soil is enough for any plant food to grow in the farm lands. Then, fruit, rice, vegetable etc. agriculture businesses will have much beneficial attribution to global farmers.

The question is how to use deep-learning technologies in the environmental field to predict the status of pro-environmental consumption. We predicted the pro-environmental consumption index based on Google search query data, using a recurrent neural network (RNN model). To certify the accuracy of the index, we compared the prediction accuracy of the RNN model with that of the ordinary least square and artificial necessary network models.

For example, the RNN model predicts the pro-environmental consumption index better than any other model. we expect the RNN model to perform still better in a big data environment because the deep-learning technologies would be increasingly as the volume of data grows. So, deep-learning technologies could be useful in environmental forecasting to prevent damage caused by climate change to influence any rice, vegetable, tomato, potato, fruit etc. different plant food grow in any countries' farming land easily.

For South Korea example, over 800 government agencies spent 2.2 trillion Korea won on eco-products in 2014 year. However, green products are rarely purchased outside these agencies. This phenomenon occurs because there is a gap between consumer attitudes and behavior , that is environmental attitude is a major factor in decision making vis-a-vis the consumption of " green" food and services (Jorea Ministry of Environment, 2015).

Therefore, it is necessary to understand those consumer

attitude, that will lead to sustainability-conductive behavior and consumption. (AI) Deep learning system can be applied to attempt understand those traveler attitude to environment protection to fly to which country. For example, (AI) deep learning system can attempt to gather data concerns how many Hong Kong people concern air pollution challenge to influence their health, then it can attempt to predict how many Hong Kong travelers do not choose to go China travel, due to the air pollution challenge to influence their health.

4.11 Environmental travel predictive consumption

Recently, many researchers have studied pro-environmental consumption and household indexes as well as suicide rate predictions using messages posted by internet users on Google trend, Tweets etc. channel.

Whether can environmental consumption be predicted by (AI) deep-learning technological internet channel to influence how many travelers choose to go to the country to travel?

How can impact the pro-environmental consumption attitudes of green policies to influence how many travelers choose to go to the country to travel?

For example, Korea scientists estimated pro-environmental attitudes using search query data provided by Google trend and confirmed through regression analysis, that pro-environmental attitude has a positive correlation with the pro-environmental attitude index. They also explained that environment-friendly attitude of residents plan an important role in policy making. In the past, most household consumption indexed were calculated through surveys, but (AI) deep-learning technological tool " big data" have recently gained research attention (Lee et al.

2016). So, (AI) deep learning technology can attempt to gather whether how many Korea residents who concern environment pollution to influence their eating green food attitude then to judge whether how many Korea residents hope to leave their country to travel anywhere either high risk environment pollution countries to travel or low risk environment pollution countries to travel in the future.

It seems that (AI) deep-learning technology can help agricultural export countries' farmers , e.g. US, UK, Canada, New Zealand, Australia, Japan, China, India etc. they can predict environmental behavioral consumption to any rice, tomato, potato , fruit, vegetable etc. plant food consumers. The beneficial advantages to them include as below:

(a) Assuming they know their countries' weather, when it has less rain to cause drought or when it has more rain in any seasonal time in the year. They can choose not to grow any kinds of above these plant food to avoid loss.

(b) They can make any kinds of above these plant food price raising after their prediction of these bad seasonal time to cause their plant food shortage supply challenge. Because these plant food consumers' demand number is more, but the supply of these above plant food supply number is less. However, due to they had predicted when the bad seasonal time can not allow them to grow these above plant food before. So, they have enough time to grow many these above plant food number in predictive good seasonal time to prepare to supply to their plant food import countries' plant food consumers to eat. Thus, these predictive environmental consumption plant food export countries can raise their plant food price to sell to them. When, the other non-pre-predictive environmental consumption plant food export countries can not supply any one of those plant food to them to eat, due to the bad climate to cause them can't grow any one of these plant food to export to sell.

Thus, (AI) deep-learning technology can be applied to predict how to raise the plant food supply number in order to raise price to the import plant food countries consumers to eat, due to they feel difficult to buy these plant food to eat in the bad climate seasonal time in whole year.

(c) (AI) deep-learning technology can help climate scientists to find what reasons cause their countries; rain sudden increases or cause their countries' rain sudden decreases. After its gathering data analysis, it can assist climate scientists to find solution methods to attempt to control the rain level can be right falling down level to let agricultural export farmers who can grow their plant food to sell to agricultural import countries in whole year.

(d) The agricultural export countries' farmers can apply (AI) deep-learning technology to help them to choose whether growing which kinds of plant food in that whether climate time to earn more plant food consumption number more easily.

Due to the agricultural countries climate will often change, for example, tomato, potato, rice, fruit etc. plant food can be adapt to grow in more rain time, but vegetable can not be adapt to grow in more rain time. If farmers can apply this technology to predict when it will have move rain or when it will have less rain to fall down in their countries. Then, they can choose to grow which kinds of plant food number more, in the suitable seasonal climate time in order to raise plant food growing number productivities to supply to sell to satisfy any agricultural food import countries' demand effectively.

(e) (AI) deep-learning technology can help agricultural import countries to solve agricultural food shortage challenge in long term. When this technology can be popular to base applied by the agricultural plant food export countries. It will solve global agricultural food shortage challenge. For example, when one agricultural export countries' farmers can popular accept to apply this technology to predict when to grow which kinds of plant food more to rise number productivities to sell. e.g. vegetable, fruit, rice Besides another agricultural export countries' farmers can also accept to apply this technology to predict when to grow plant food, e.g. potato, tomato to raise number productivities to sell. Then, they can concentrate on growing the specific kinds of plant food in order to raise the specific plant food number productivities in every seasonal change time every month. Then, global agricultural plant food supply must be raised, due to these predictive environmental change farmers can know who ought grow which kinds of plant food to sell to raise number productivities.

Consequently, (AI) deep learning can gather where countries will have high risk environment pollution to influence health food supply. Then, it can give opinions to travelling businesses when these high risk environment pollution countries will encounter the traveler number to be decreased, due to the environment pollution serious challenge will occur.

4.12 What methods can predict future travel behavioral consumption ?

How to use qualitative of travel behavioral method to predict future travel consumption from (AI) big data ?

I also suggest to use qualitative of travel behavioral method to predict future travel consumption. Methods such as focus groups interviews and participant observer techniques can be used with quantitative approaches on their own to fill the gaps left by quantitative techniques. These insights have contributed to the development of increasingly sophisticated models to forecast travel behavior and predict changes in behavior in response to change in the transportation system. I shall indicate the weaknesses of human travelling investigation methods as below:

First, survey methods restrict not only the question frame but the answer frame as well, anticipating the important issues and questions and the responses. However, these surveys methods are not well suited to exploratory areas of research where issues remain unidentified and the researched seek to answer the question "why?".

Second, data collection methods using traditional travel diaries or telephone recruitment can under represent certain segments of the population, particularly the older persons with little education, minorities and the poor. Before the survey, focus group for example can be used to identify what socio-demographic variables to include in the survey, how best to structure the diary, even what incentives will be most effective in increasing the response rate.

After the survey, focus, focus groups can be used to build explanations for the survey results to identify the "why" of the results as well as the implications. One Asia Pacific survey research result was made by tourism market investigation before. It indicated the travel in Asia Pacific market in the past, had often been undertaken in large groups through leisure package sold in bulk, or in large organized business groups, future travelers will be in smaller groups or alone, and for a much wider range of reasons.

Significant new traveler segments, such as female business traveler. The small business traveler and the senior traveler, all of which have different aspirations and requirements from the travel experience.

Moreover, Asia tourism market will start to exist behaviors in the adoption of newer technologies, a giving the traveler new ways to manage the travel experience, creating new behaviors. This with provide new opportunities for travel providers. The use of mobile devices, smartphones, tablets etc. and social media are the obvious findings to become an integral part of the travel experience. Thus, quality method can attempt to predict Asia Pacific tourism market development in the future. It is such as (AI) big data gathering tool can give traveler quality opinions to any travelling businesses to make the more accurate where will be the popular travel destination choice next month or next half year or next year.

However, improving the predictive power of travel behavior models and to increase understanding travel behavior which lies in the use of panel data(repeated measures from the same individuals). Whereas, cross-sectional data only reveal inter-individual differences at one moment in time, panel data can reveal intra-individual changes over time. In effect, panel data are generally better suited to understand and predict (changes in) travel behavior. However, a substantial proportion was also observed to transition between very different activity/ travel patterns over time, indicating that from one year to the next, many people renegotiated their activity/travel patterns.

4.13 How to apply advanced traveler information systems (ATIS) to predict future travelling behavior?

Nowadays, information can impact on traveler behavior and network performance. For example, when steadily growing levels of vehicle ownership and vehicle miles traveled information has been identified as a potential strategy towards man aging travel demand, optimizing transportation networks and better utilizing available capacity. Toward, this goal to predict further tourist behavioral consumption. Many countries, government tourism development institutes has applied advanced traveler information systems (ATIS) which travel behavior models and high-fidelity network performance models made increasingly feasible through the rapid advances in computer power. Crucial components of this problem domain are the modeling of individual tourist drivers' response to travel information and the development accurate guidance of relevance to real would trip makers. So, this advanced traveler information systems (ATIS) can assist the tourist who like to rent travelling car tools to travel in any countries own free traveler information systems service conveniently. Also, this travel information system can be intended to assist travelers to make better travel choices. e.g. this system can improve the decision making of individual traveler rather than improvements of network performance overall. So, we need to understand how tourists make their travel plans. Also, understanding decision process that lead to booking of the trip is equally important, as it allows of a potential behavior.

4.14 How can online tourism sale channel influence traveling consumption of behavior?

Nowadays, internet is popular, it seems that booking air ticket behavior of using internet is predicted to influence overall tourism air tickets payment method. Tourism industry has grown in the previous several decades. Despite its global impact, questions related to better understanding of tourists and whose habits. Using online travel air ticket booking benefits include booking electronic air tickets can be made from entering any electronic travel agents websites in the short time and electronic travel ticket payers do not need leave home, who can pay visa card to pre booking any electronic travel ticket from online channel conveniently.

How can analyze activity based travel demand ?

Nowadays, human are concerning the traffic congestion and air quality deterioration, the supply oriented focus of transportation planning has expanded to include how to manage travel demand within the available transportation supply. Consequently, there has been an increasing interest in travel demand management strategies, such as congestion pricing that attempts to change aggregate travel demand. The prediction aggregate level, long term travel demand to understanding disaggregate level (i.e. individual levels) behavioral responses to short term demand policies, such as ride sharing incentives, congestion pricing and employer based demand management schemes, alternate work schedules, telecommuting limitation of travel agent traditionally work nature shall influence oriented trip based travel modelling passenger travel demand indirectly.

Finally, online travel purchase will be popular to influence the number of travel behavioral consumption nowadays. Any travel package products can be sold from websites to attract travelers to choose to pre-book air ticket for any trips conveniently. In the past ten years, the internet has become the predominant carrier of all types of information and transactions. Regarding travel decisions, internet has also become an important sales channels for the travel industry, because it is associated with comparably lower distribution and sales costs, but also because it adapts to high supply and demand dynamics in this industry. Consequently, the travel and tourism industry tries to increase the internet sale specific share of sales volumes. So, internet sale channel has changed travel consumption behavioral pattern and characteristics and travel experience. For example, Switzerland has one of the highest population-to-computer ratio in Europe. It is also one of the most highly internet penetrated countries in terms of use of the WWW on a day-to-day basis, with more than 75 percent of the population older than 14 years using the WWW daily (ICT, 2005).

The reason of booking online tourism may include: convenience, fast transaction, finding traveling package choice easily, more airline seats available. So, online booking tourism will influence the traditional tourism agents visiting of sales and air tickets and travelling package numbers to be decreased. Finally, the online booking tourism market shares will be expanded to more than traditional tourism agents visits sale market in the future one day. So, the travel agents who still use the traditional tourism visiting sale channel which ought raise whose features to compare to differ to online tourism sale channel if these traditional tourism agents want to keep competitive ability in tourism industry for long term.

What is actively based patterns of urban population of travel behavioral prediction method?

Actively based patterns of urban population. It is a method of motivational framework means in which societal constraints and inherent individual motivations interact to shape activity participation patterns. It can be used to predict one city or urban the numbers of travel demand in the year. It has two elements: First, capability constraints refer to constraints are imposed by biological needs, such as eating and sleeping and/or resources, such as income, availability of cars etc. to undertake the urban or city's family activities in the year. Second, coupling constraints define where, when and the duration of planning activities that are to be pursued with other individuals. So, this method needs to gather information (data) to get the relationship between activities, travel and spending work time and space time to evaluate whether there are how many families who have real needs to spend time to go to travel in the year.

What is trip based versus activity based approaches?

What is trip based versus activity based approaches? The fundamental difference between the trip-based and activity based approaches is that the former approach directly focuses on trips without explicit recognition of the motivation or reason for the trips and travel. The activity based approach , on the other hand, views travel as a demand derived from the need to pursue travel activities. So, it is better understand the individual or family behavior basis for individual or family travelling decision regarding participation in travelling activities in certain places or cities or countries at given times and hence the resulting travel needs. This behavioral basis includes all the factors that influence the why, how, when and where of performed activities and resulting individuals and household, the cultural/social norms of the community and the travel surrounding environment.

Another difference between the two approaches is in the way travel is represented. The trip based approach represents travel as a collection of trips. Each trip is considered as independent of other trips, without considering the inter-relationship in the choice attributes , such as time, destination and mode of different trips. As tours are chains of trips beginning and ending at a same location , say home or work. The tour based representation helps maintain the consistency across and capture the interdependency and consistency of the modeled choice attributed among the trips of the same tour.

In addition to the tour based representation of travel, the activity based approach focuses on sequences or patterns of activity participation and travel behavior, using the whole day or longer periods of time is the unit of analysis. Such as approach can address travel demand management issues through an examination of how people modify their activity participation, for example, will individuals substitute more out-of-home activities for in home activities in the evening of who arrived early form work due-to a work schedule change?

The major difference between trip based and the activity based approaches is in the way, the time dimension of activities and travel is considered. In the trip based approach, time is reduced to being simply a cost making a trip and a day's viewed as a combination, defined peak and off peak time periods. On the other hand, activity based approach views individuals' activity travel patterns are a result of their time use decisions with a continuous time domain. As individuals have 24 hours in a day or multiples of 24 hours for longer periods of time and decide how to use that travel among or allocate that time to activities and travel and with who, subject to their socio-demographic, transportation system and other and scheduling of trips. So, determining the impact of travel demand management policies on time use behavior is an important step to assessing the impact of such policies on individual travel behavior. The final major difference between this two approaches relates to the level of aggregation. In the trip based approach, most aspect of travel, e.g. number of trips etc. are analyzed at an aggregate level.

Consequently, trip based methods accommodate the effect of socio-demographic attributes of households and individuals in a very limited fashion, which limits the activity of the method to evaluate travel impacts of long term socio-demographic characteristics of the individuals who actually make the activity travel choices and the travel service characteristics of the surrounding environment. So, the activity based models are better equipped to forecast the longer term changes in travel demand in response composition and the travel environment of urban areas. Also, using activity based models, the impact of policies can be assessed by predicting individual level behavioral responses instead of employing trip based statistical averages that are aggregated over defined demographic segments.

4.15 Can apply (AI) big data gathering method predict senior age will be main travelling target?

In the past, Germany government had established tourism survey analysis to analyze survey data in order to arrive at reliable conclusions on future trends in travel behavior. To aim to find how demographic change will influence the tourism market and how the industry can adapt to those changes. The travel analysis provided data on tourism consumer behavior, including attitudes, motives and intentions. Since, 1970 year, it is based on a random sample, representative for the population in private households aged 14 years or older. Then, a continuous high scientific standard combined with a national and international users makes the travel analysis a useful tool and reliable source for tourism industry and policy decisions. It aimed to gather statistical data. e.g. on the age structure and on demographic trends, quantitative and qualitative analysis with time series data from the travel analysis. It shows e.g. not only the future volume , quite different from today's seniors, or how who will travel of family holidays will change, e.g. single parents of low, but grandparents of growing significance for tourism.

Demographic change is said to be one of the important drivers for new trends in consumer traveling change behavior in most European countries (e.g. Lind 2001). Because the growing number of senior citizens in the European Union and other industrialized countries, such as the USA and Japan, looks to become one of the major marketing challenges for the tourism industry. United Nations statistics predict that the share of people being 60 age or older will grow dramatically in the coming future, and is expected to rise from 10 percent of the world population in 2000 year to more than 20 percent in 2050 year (United Nations Population Division, 2001). From its statistic, some data showed that travel propensity increased throughout life until the age of about 50 years of age and was then kept stable until very late in life 75 age. The most important results is that the travel propensity when getting older is not going down between 65 and 75 age of course, the overall development of this variable is influenced by a lot of other factors which are responsible for quite a variation over time. It is now possible to suggest that the general pattern of travel propensity is one of the key indicators for holiday life cycle travel behavior, includes three stages. The growth stage tends to increase from early adult hood until 45 age old or when reaching some 80%. The next stage is stabilization from the ages of around 50 age, until 75 age old, starting with a lower increase. Finally, the decrease stage is a slight decrease occurs once people reach the more advanced age of 75 age to 85 age old (Lohmann & Danielsson 2001).

So, it seems Germany government tourism prediction to future travelers' behavior indicated these findings, such as on how future senior generations will travel, who had used survey data to examine the patterns of travel behavior of a generation getting older and applied the findings to draw conclusions on the future. Also, it predicted that on the future of family trips, family segmentation will be the travel behavior patterns in the future. These findings together with the statistical data on demographic change allowed for a better understanding of the coming tends in family holidays. It's aim developed in consumer behavior related to demographic change and predicted what will happen future of tourism one had to consider other influences and drivers as well, for example, trends on the supply side. e.g. low cost airlines or in travelling consumption behavior in general whether how the past may provide a key to predict travel patterns of senior citizens to the future.

Given the projected growth of the senior citizens market, designing specific marketing strategies to meet the prospective needs of elderly tourists will become increasingly important. It has been an implicit assumption that it will be a close relationship between the travel behavior of today's senior citizens and the those of future ones. The growing number of senior citizens in the world. e.g. China, Hong Kong, Japan, USA etc. countries. Global senior citizen tourism market will be based solely on demographic predictions about the future of the population's age structure. However, many of these seniors won't only live longer but will be fitter and more active until later in life. Many of the will also have plenty in life. Many of them will also have plenty of time and money to spend on travel. So, will these new seniors behave like today's senior citizens? Will they adopt the same travel behavior as the previous generation or become a new market of oldies for the leisure and tourism industry? However, to determine the actual number of senior citizens who will be travelling and to sought to evaluate and specify certain difficult to predict the actual numbers of senior citizen to any country. However, they can be based on the implicit assumption that there is a close relationship between the travel behavior of past, present and future seniors. But is this a valid assumption? As the revise-analysis travel analysis survey, which was conducted in Germany every year, offered some interesting data possibilities. It was designed to monitor the holiday travel behavior, opinions and attitudes of Germans and has been carried out since 1970 year, questions in the questionnaire. Data are based on face to face interviews, with a representative sample of more than 7,500 respondents, the interviews being carried out in January each year. All results refer to the average for the defined generated, which ranges generally over ten years. The group of people then at the age of 60 to 69 age is described. This corresponds to the same generation ten years ago, when they had an age of 50 to 59 age. When this methodological approach is not necessarily very sophisticated, it does have the important advantages of being cost effective.

IS (AI) big data gathering method a better psychological method to compare human marketing research method predict travel behavioral consumption?

On the psychological view point, I think individual traveler's character will have those kind of personal characteristics. First, simplicity searchers value above everything ease not transparency in their travel planning and holiday making, and are willing to avoid having to go through extensive research. Second, cultural purists use their travel as an opportunity to immerse themselves in an unfamiliar looking to break themselves entirely from their home lives and engage. Sincerely with a different way of living. Third, social capital seekers understand that to be well travelled is a personal quality, and their choices are shaped by their desire to take maximum of social reward from their travel. They will exploit the potential of digital media to enrich and inform their experiences, and structure their adventures always keeping in mind they are being watched by online audiences. Finally, reward hunters seek a return on the investment who make in their busy , high-achieving lives. Linked in part to the growing trend of wellness, including both physical and mental self-improvement who seek truly extraordinary and often indulgent or luxurious' must have experiences.

Why needs to know the personal character of individual traveler's characteristics? Because if travel agents could feel which kinds of individual traveler's character, then who can predict which kind of travel package to design to them more easily. For example, how to determine future travel behavior from past travel experience and perceptions of risk and safety? We need to concern that the influences of past international travel experience, types of risk associated with international travel and the overall degree of safety feeling during international travel on individual's travelling experiences likelihood of travelling to various geographic regions on their next international vacation trip or avoidance of those regions, due to perceived risk. Because individual traveler's experience of safety risk degree to the countries, it will influence who chooses to go to the countries/country to travel again.

Why travelers avoid certain destinations are as relevant decision making as why who choose to go to the country(countries) to travel. Perceptions of risk and safety and travel experiences are likely to influence travel decisions; efforts to predict future travel behavior can benefit to individual tourist's decision making.

As Weber & Bottorn (1989) defined risky decision is as "choices among alternatives that can be described by probability distributions over possible outcomes" (p.114). Some psychologists judge subjective perceptions of physical reality, i.e. image of a particular tourist destination, whereas value judgement refers to the way individual rank destinations according to whose attributes. i.e. attractiveness, safety, risk etc. factors to form on overall image. So, if the individual traveler had unhappy and worried and unsafe experiences to go to where the place(country) to travel during whose vacation time before. Then, this negative travel experience will influence who is afraid to go to the place (country) to travel again. Risk of place, country, destination or region means the danger is relatively high to the place, i.e. increasing in airplane accidents, crime or terrorist activity targeting citizens of potential traveler's nationality or the probability of occurrence is great , i.e. recent occurrences involving travel regions/destinations under consideration or effective actions to control consequences exist. i.e. selecting safe regions and destinations, taking extra precautions when traveling to risky destinations. These risk factors will influence the individual traveler who chooses to cancel travel plan to go to the country again.

Another interesting research, how to predict behavioral intention of choosing a travel destination, which has focus of tourism research for years, but the complex decision making process leading to the choice of a travel destination has not been well researched. The planned behavior model using its core constructs, attitude, subjective norm and perceived behavioral control, with the addition of the past behavioral variable on behavioral intention of choosing a travel destination.

Understanding why people travel and what factors influence their behavioral intention of choosing a travel destination is beneficial to tourism planning and marketing. Understanding travel motivation is the push and pull model. The idea of the push and pull model is the decomposition of an individual's choice of a travel destination into two forces. The first force is the push factor that pushes an individual away home and attempts to develop a general desire to go somewhere else, without specifying where that may be. The second force is the pull factor, that pulls on individual toward a destination, due to a region specific travel location or perceived attractiveness of a destination. The respective push and pull factors illustrate that people travel because who are pushed by their internal motives and pulled by external forces of a destination. Nevertheless, how push and pull factors guide people's attitude and how these attributes lead to behavioral intentions of choosing a travel destination have rarely been investigated. The decision making process leading to the choice of a travel destination is a very complex process. The planned behavior model is as a research framework to predict the behavioral intention of choosing a travel destination. The model based on the three constructs of attitude, subjective norm, and perceived behavioral control (Fishbein & Ajzen, 1975).

In conclusion, the factors can influence travelers who decide to choose to travel the country, which include personal safety was perceived to the highest motivation factors among the important factors which include, scenic beauty, cultural interests, friendliness of local people, price of trip, services in hotels and restaurants, quality and variety of food and shopping facilities and services. The factors include both push and pull. Push factors include knowledge, prestige, and enhancement of human relationship etc., whereas, the most significant pull factors include high technologic image, expenditure and accessibility etc. For example, Japanese travelers visiting Hong Kong. Push factors are such as exploration dream fulfillment and pull factors are such as benefits sought, attractions and good climate city. It will be the factor of future travel patterns and motivations of sub-cultural and ethic groups for Japanese choice to go to Hong Kong travelling.

4.16 How can apply (AI) digital channel (big data gathering method) predict travelling consumer behaviors?

(AI) big data digital channel can be applied to help travelling businesses to evaluate whether how much the e-ticket price and travelling package price is the most attractive or reasonable to persuade travelling consumers feel it is the most reasonable price to choose to buy the airline's e-tickets or the travel agent's travelling package product from internet channel . It helps travelling consumers to feel which airlines or travelling agents which ought change their e-ticket and/or travelling package price to let travelling consumers to choose to buy the airline e-ticket or the travelling agent's travelling package products from internet channel. It can be applied to predict whether how many travelling consumer numbers can be increased or decreased when the airline e-ticket price is variable or the travelling agent travelling package price is variable . It aims to give opinions to help any online airlines or travelling agents to judge whether which e-ticket or travelling package price is the most reasonable to let travelling consumers to accept to choose to buy which airline's e-tickets or traveling agent's package products more attractive.

Thus, (AI) e-ticket or e-travelling package price measurement technology can be preference to be applied online communication ecommerce and mobile phone internet platform aspect. As traveling businesses can enter their past e-ticket or travelling package prices data and past travelling customer number data into computer or mobile. Then, (AI) price measurement technology can gather these data to analyze these e-ticket or travelling package product prices and past travelling customer number to compare their e-ticket and/or travelling package prices variable changing range level to find their e-ticket and /or travelling package price variable difference to measure to make conclusion about every travelling package or/and e-ticket product's price variable changing will influence how many travelling customer number increase or decrease changing to choose to sell their different kinds of travelling package or e-ticket products more accurate. Then, (AI) price measurement software will help them to analyze all past e-ticket and/or travelling package price variable changing data to compare whether which e-ticket and/or travelling package price range can let travelling customers to feel it is more reasonable and attractive to influence them to choose to buy their e-ticket or travelling package product among different airlines and travel agent choices. Because any e-ticket or travelling package product's price is one important factor to influence travelling consumers to choose to buy the airline's e-tickets or travelling agent's travelling package products.

For example, Amazon publish has applied (AI) price measurement technology to help authors to decide how much every different topic of e-book or paper book price, it can attract the largest number of readers to buy. Any one author only needs to type whose book name to Amazon publish author himself/herself Amazon website. Amazon publish (AI) price measurement learning machine will help them to auto-calculate and judge how much e-book or paper book price is the most attractive and the most reasonable in order to increase reader number to buy their e-books or paper books to read. So, (AI) online price measurement machine will gather past similar book names and past every similar book readers' reading times and the number of readers to give opinions to let every author to judge whether his/her very new e-book or paper book ought charge how much price to the e-book or paper book which can attract many readers to choose to buy. Although, it is not ensure that the e-book or paper book price must let readers to feel it is the most reasonable price to choose to buy in reader's view point. However, it has other factors to influence readers' choice to buy the e-book or paper book, e.g. whether the book content is attractive to public, the author's familiarity, the book's page is enough or not to satisfy readers to read etc. factors. But, instead of all these extra factors to influence readers to choose to buy the book to read. (AI) price measurement learning machine can real give opinions to every author to let them to judge the e-book or paper book different price range whether is too high to influence readers to choose to buy to read or tool low to influence readers feel it is possible poor content book to compare other similar content books. Thus, (AI) price measurement machine can help authors to predict every reader's reading behaviors or reading experience and reading habit from online channel in short time easily. The author only enter the book name to let Amazon publish price measurement machine to check, it will follow past reader's reading habit and reading experience to judge whether the similar all book topic sale record to judge how much price is the reasonable price to attract many readers to buy the book.

Hence, (AI) can be applied to digital channel to help travelling businesses to predict travelling consumer behavior in the future. In the future, mobile/smartphone, laptop, desktop will be most frequent used ecommerce channels to develop online business. So, (AI) can be also applied to these platforms to gather data to make analysis to help travelling businesses to predict travelling consumer purchase behaviors popularly. Due to , ecommerce is popular to global, so digital online and instore channels can be one good channel to let (AI) learning machine to make platform to gather past every online travelling consumer purchase (buying) experience data to help travelling businesses to build airline or travelling agent brand personality and having a responsible, positive impact on society.

To apply (AI) learning machine technology to understand

travelling customer online purchase behavior, it will raise business e-commerce successful chance: For example, (AI) learning machine can help travelling businesses to gather data to analyze to determine whether short-term or long-term signals in the online travelling consumer behavior that indicate higher purchase intents to let every online travelling business to know. (AI) learning machine can find that online users with long-term purchasing intent tend to save and click through on more content.

However, as online travelling users approach the time of purchase their activity becomes more topically focused and actions shift from saves to searches from online travelling consumption channel. Then, (AI) learning machine will further find that the brand airline and/or travelling agent purchase signals in online travelling consumption behavior can exist weakness before an online travelling purchase is made and can also be traced across different online travelling purchase categories. Finally, (AI) learning machine synthesize these insights in predictive models of online travelling user purchasing intent to the brand of airline or/and travelling agent travelling package product. Taken together, it's work identifies a set of general principles and signals that can be used to model online travelling user e-ticket and/or travelling package purchasing intent across many online content discovery applications. Thus, (AI) learning machine can help online travelling businesses to gather any online travelling users' click online travelling behaviors data to judge whether there are how many online travelling users will choose to find their online travelling business websites to make final decisions to buy their travelling package or/and e-ticket products from online channels. Then, it will give opinions to help the online travelling businesses to let it to judge whether what are the important website factors will help its online travelling business to attract many online travelling consumers, e.g. designing unattractive travelling website issue, online unattractive scene photos issue, unclear website travelling photo color issue, unclear website travelling advertisement message, contents and words impressions issue, lacking image movement frequent attractive seeing issue etc. different website factors. Thus, online digital channel will be one good choice to apply (AI) learning machine to help travelling businesses to predict travelling consumer behaviors.

Thus, (AI) big data technology can also assist travelling consumers to gather different manufacturers' data to compare what their advantages and disadvantages of their travelling package products are. Then, travelling consumers can make comparison to choose which airline or travelling agent is the suitable to whom to buy e-ticket or pre-booking travelling package in online travelling consumption market.

.

Thus, I believe that artificial intelligent "big data" gathering method can be suggested to be applied to attempt to predict travelling consumer behavioral changes in global online travelling business environment, the reasons are as below:
On the travelling consumer's beneficial hand, travelling consumers can apply this (AI) big data gathering method to attempt to gather any global airline e-tickets and/or travelling agent's package product data to be analyzed by this artificial intelligent learning system to compare human general marketing research method, e.g. survey, questionnaire, marketing plan etc. different human

judgement methods to predict traveler consumption behavioral change model. Then, it analyzed all the different data to compare what are the range of the most reasonable e-ticket and/or travelling package online purchase history and sale in order to make more accurate prediction to future traveler change traveling consumption behavioral model in next month, or next half year or next year short term period traveling consumption change prediction. Thus, it seems that future AI tool can be attempted to apply to predict any industries price behavior, e.g. deciding what level of price is the attractive level to attract consumer in these industries, e.g. fuel, education, tourism, health, entertainment, etc. different product purchase. It can give more absolute price suggestion to any merchants to set their price change predict in order to increase many customer numbers to buy their products in every year, or every quarter every month, or month week, even every day etc. different sale period.

Reference

Backman and others "motivation is conceptually viewed as " a state of need, a condition that services as a driving force to display different kind of behavior toward certain types of activities, developing preferences, arriving at some expected satisfactory outcome.", 1995, p.15.

Fishbein & Ajzen, "The model based on the three constructs of attitude, subjective norm, and perceived behavioral control". 1975.

Hsu et al. "A tourist behavior model has been developed, called the expectation, motivation and attitude " (EMA) model ,2010.

ICT,WWW . "Switzerland has one of the highest population-to-computer ratio in Europe." Switzerland,

2005.

Jorea Ministry of Environment, " For South Korea environmental attitude is a major factor in decision making vis-a-vis the consumption of " green" food and services", Korea, 2015.

Korea Ministry Of Environment. Public Organizations spend 2.2 Trillon Korean Won To
Purchase green Products in 2014; Ministry Of Environment: Sejoung, Korea, 2015.

Lind , Lohmann & Danielsson , United Nations Population Division, "Demographic change is said to be one of the important drivers for new trends in consumer traveling change behavior in most European countries". 2001.

Mayne, Lonnie. " Evolve of die in the age of the consumer". Entrepreneur, N.P. , 16 Apr. 2014. web of Oct. 2016.

Lee, D.; Kim, M. ; Lee, J. adoption of green electricity policies: Investigating the role of environmental attitudes via big data-driven search-queries. Energy policy 2016. 90, 187-201.

Lee, Terrence, " Tech in Asia-connecting Asia's startup system " Tech. in Asia- connecting Asia's startup ecosystem, N.p.,4 July 2016.

Weber & Bottorn "risky decision is as choices among alternatives that can be described by probability distributions over possible outcomes" , 1989, p.114.

CHAPTER IV

What factors can influence travel behavioural consumption

Prediction travel behavioral consumption from traditional human's mind of tourism market research method

How to predict travel consumption? It is one question to any travel agents concern to use what methods which can predict how many numbers of travelers where who will choose to go to travel more accurately. I think that who can consider how to predict travel behavioral consumption from psychology view and computer science view both.

On the psychology view, It has evidence to support the relationship between self-identify threat and resistance to change travel behavior to any travelers, controlling for whose past travelling behavior, resistance to change if a psychological phenomenon of long standing interest in many applied branches of psychology. Past travelling behavior has been acknowledged as a predictor of future action. Such as travelling behavior that is experienced as successful is likely to be repeated and may lead to habitual patterns. Some psychologists differentiate habit between two concepts, such as goal oriented and automatic oriented both. Although repeated past travelling behavior is addition goal oriented and automatic oriented. Further non-deliberative nature of habit may make appeals to judge and to predict future individual traveler's behaviour accrately. However, repeated travelling behavior without a necessary constraint of goal orientation and automatic oriented both.

So, it seems that psychological factor can influence any individual traveler why and how who choose to decide whose travelling behaviour.

On the computer statistic view, structural equation modeling is an extremely flexible linear-in-parameters multivariate statistical modeling technique. It has been used in modeling travel behavior and values since about 1980 year. It is a software method to handle a large number of variables, as well as unobserved variables specified as linear combinations (weighted averages) of the observed variable.

Whether climate change can influence travelling behaviours.

The flexibility of human travelling behavior is at least the result of one such mechanism, our ability to travel mentally in time and entertain potential future. Understanding of the impacts is holidays, particularly those involving travel. Using focus groups research to explores tourists' awareness of the impacts of travel own climate change, examines the extent to which climate change features in holiday travel decisions and identifies some of the barriers to the adoption of less carbon intensive tourism practices. The findings suggest many tourists don't consider climate change when planning their holidays. The failure of tourists to engage with the climate change to impact of holidays, combined with significant barriers to behavioral change, presents a considerable challenge in the tourism industry.

Tourism is a highly energy intensive industry and has only recently attracted attention as an important contributions to climate change through greenhouse gas emissions. It has been estimated that tourism contributes 5% of global carbon dioxide emissions. There have been a number of potential changes proposed for reducing the impact of air travel on climate change. These include technological changes, market based changes and behavioral changes. However, the role that climate change plays in the holiday and travel decisions of global tourists. How the global tourists of the impacts travel has on climate change to establish the extent to which climate change, considerations features in holiday travel decision making processes and to investigate the major barriers to global tourists adopting less carbon intensive travel practices. Whether tourists will aware the impacts that their holidays and travel have on climate changes.

When, it comes to understand indvidual traveler's behavioral change, wide range of conceptual theories have been developed, utilizing various social, psychological, subjective and objective variables in order to model travel consumption behavior. These theories of travel behavioral change operate at a number of different levels, including the individual level, the interpersonal level and community level. Whether pro-environmental behavior can be used to predict travel consumption behavior in a climate change. However, the question of what determines pro-environmental behavior in such a complex one that it can not be visualized through one single framework or diagram.

Despite the potentially high risk scenario for the tourism industry and the global environment, the tourism and climate change ought have close relationship. Whether what are the important factors and variables which can limit tourism? e.g. money, time, family problem, extreme hot or cold weather change, air ticket price, journey attraction etc. variable factors. Mention of holidays and travel were deliberately avoided in the recruitment process, so as not to create a connection factor to influence traveler's individual mind. However, the dismissal of alternative transportation modes can be conceived as either a structural barrier, in the sense that flying is perhaps the only realistic option to reach long-haul holiday destination, or a perceived behavioral control barriers in that an individual perceives flying as the only option open to whom. The transportation tool factor will be depend to extent on the distance to the destination. This can also be interpreted in a social perspective as an intention with the resources available where much international tourism is structured around flying. To increase the availability of different transportation modes, tourists could choose holiday destination closer to home.

Finally, also how to predict future travel behavioural consumption. I feel that travel agents need to predict whether any country's random daily variation of weather factor is also important to influence travel behaviour. e.g. in weather, temperature, rainfall adn snowfall with traffic accidents factors will have relationship to cause travel demand. Some scientists estimate suggest that when warmed temperatures and reduced snowfall are associated with a moderate decline in non-fatal accidents, they are also associated with a significant increase in fatal accidents. Thus increase in fatalities and temperature. Half of the estimated effect of temperature on fatalities is due to changes in the exposure to pedestrians, bicyclists and motorcyclists as temperature increase. So, if any countries have rainfall, snowfall and low temperature to cause traffic accidents, whether this accident occurrence will influence the travelers who liking climb snow hills, riding bicycle, running sports who will avoid to travel to these countries' bad weather after occurs. So, why I feel that this natural climate factor will also be one serious factor to influence travel behavioral consumption.

Market method predicts future travel consumption behavior

Whether individual habitual behaviour can influence travelling behaviour : e.g. renting travel transportation tools

Whether habit can be intended to predict of future travel behavior to people are creatures of habits. Many of human's everyday goal-directed behaviors are performed in a habitual fashion, the transportation made and route one takes to work, one's choice of breakfast. Habits are formed when using the some behavior frequently and a similar consistency in a similar context for the some purpose whether the individual past travel consumption model will be caused a habit to whom. e.g. choosing whom travel agent to buy air ticket or traveling package; choosing the same or similar countries' destinations to go to travel ; choosing the business class or normal (general) class of quality airlines to catch planes. Does habitual rent traveling car tools use not lead to more resistance to change of travel mode? It has been argued that past behavior is the best predictor of future behavior to travel consumption. If individual traveler's past consumption behavior was always reasoned, then frequency of prior travel consumption behavior should only have an indirect link to the individual traveler's behavior. It seems that renting travel car tools to use is a habit example. So, a strong rent traveling car tools useful habit makes traveling mode choice. People with a strong renting of traveling car tools of habit should have low motivation to attend to gather any information about public transportation in their choice of travelling country for individual or family or friends members during their traveling journeys.

Even when persuasive communication changes the traveler whose attitudes and intention, in the case of individual traveler or family travelers with a strong renting travel car tools habit. It is difficult to change whose travel behaviors to choose to catch public transportation in whose any trips in any countries. However, understanding of travel behavior and the reasons for choosing one mode of transportation over another. The arguments for rent traveling car tools to use, including convenience, speed, comfort and individual freedom and well known. Increasingly, psychological factors include such as, perceptions, identity, social norms and habit are being used to understand travel mode choice. Whether how many travel consumers will choose to rent traveling car tools during their trips in any countries. It is difficult to estimate the numbers. As the average level of renting travel car tools of dependence or attitudes to certain travel package policies from travel agents. Instead different people must be treated in different ways because who are motivated in different ways and who are motivated by different travel package policies ways from travel agents.

In conclusion, the factors influence whose traveler's individual behavior either who chooses to rent traveling car tools or who chooses to catch public transportation when who individual goes to travel in alone trip or family trip. It include influence mode choice factors, such as social psychology factor and marketing on segmentation factor both to influence whose transportation choice of behavior in whose trip.

How to determine future travel behavior from past travel experience and perceptions of risk and safety for the benefits to travel consumers?

How to determine future travel behavior from past travel experience and perceptions of risk and safety for the benefits to travel consumers? Why does individual traveler avoid certain destination(s) is(are) as relevant to tourist decision making as why who chooses to travel to others. Perceptions of risk and safety and travel experience are likely to influence travel decisions. If travel agents had efforts to predict future travel behavior to guess whether travelers will feel where is(are) risk and unsafe to cause who does not choose to go to the country to travel. Then, the travel agents will avoid to choose to spend much time to design the different traveling package to attract their potential travel consumers to choose to travel. The reason is because in the case of individual traveler's tourism experience, the traveler whose past disappointment travel experience (psychological risk) will be a serious threat to the traveler's health or life (health, physical or terrorism risk). The past safety or unhealthy risk to the country(countries) will influence the traveler decides to choose not to go to the countries(country) to travel again in the future.

What is push and pull factors to influence any traveler who chooses where is whose preferable travelling destination

How to predict individual traveler's behavioral intention of choosing a travel destination. Understanding why people travel and what factors influence their behavioral intention of choosing a travel destination is beneficial to tourism planning and marketing. In general, an individual's choice of a travel destination into two forces. The first force is the push factor that pushes an individual away from home and attempt to develop a general desire to go somewhere, without specifying where that may be. The other force is the pull factor that pull an individual toward in destination, due to a region-specific or perceived attractiveness of a destination. The respective push and pull factors illustrate that people travel because who are pushed by whose internal motives and pulled by external forced of a destination. However, the decision making process leading to the choice of a travel destination is a very complex process. For example, a Taiwanese traveler who might either choose new travel destination of Hong Kong or another old travel Asia destinations again or who also might choose any one of Western country, as a new travel destination. The travel agents can predict where who will have intention to choose to travel from whose past behavior and attitude, subjective and perceived behavioral control model.

The factors influence where is the traveler choice, include personal safety, scenic beauty, cultural interest, climate changing, transportation tools, friendliness of local people, price of trip, trip package service in hotels and restaurants, quality and variety of food and shopping facilities and services etc. needs. So, whose factors will influence where is the individual travel's choice. It seems every traveler whose choice of travel process, will include past behavior. e.g. travelling experience, travelling habit, then to choose the best seasoned travelling action to satisfy whose travel needs. This process is the individual traveler's psychological choice process, who must need time to gather information to compare concerning of different travel packages, destination scene, climate change, transportation tools available to the destination, air ticket price etc. these factors, then to judge where is the best right destination to travel in the right time.

Why expectation, motivation and attitude factor can influence travelling behaviour.

Social psychology is concerned with gaining insight into the psychological of socially relevant behaviors and the processes. For instance, on a global level bad influence to global warming, it influences some countries extreme cold or hot bad climate changing occurrence, then it ought influence some travelers' behavioral decision to change their mind to choose some countries to go to travel at the moment which do not occur extreme hot or cold climate (temperature). e.g. above than 40 degree in summer or below than 0 degree in winter. Due to the extreme climate changing environment in the countries, it will cause them to feel uncomfortable to play during their trips. So, the global warming causes to climate changing factor will influence the numbers of travel consumption to be reduced possibly. This is global climate changing environment factor influences to bad or uncomfortable social psychological feeling to global travelers' mind of traveling decision. What is individual traveler expectation, motivation and attitude? Tourism sector includes inbound (domestic) tourism and outbound (overseas) tourism both incomes to any countries. According to recent article, a tourist behavior model has been developed, called the expectation, motivation and attitude (EMA) model (Hsu et al., 2010).

This model focuses on the pre-visit stage of tourists by modeling the behavioral process by incorporating expectation, motivation and attitude. Travel motivation is considered as an essential component of the behavioral process, which has been increasing attention from the travel; industry. The economic approach defines "tourism" is an identifiable nationally important industry. It includes the component activities of transportation, accommodation, recreation, food and related service. So, tourism behavioral consumption is concerned the individual tourist's usual habituate of the industry which responds to whose needs, and of the impacts that both the tourist and the tourism industry have on the socio-cultural, economic and physical environment.

However, travel motivation means how to understand and predict factors that influence travel decision making. According to Backman and others (1995, p.15), motivation is conceptually viewed as " a state of need, a condition that services as a driving force to display different kind of behavior toward certain types of activities, developing preferences, arriving at some expected satisfactory outcome." So, motivation and expectancy which has close relationship to any tourist before who decided to do any tourism of behavior. Some economists confirmed motivation and expectancy which has relations, such as expectation of visiting an outbound destination has a direct effect on motivation to visit the destination; motivation has a direct effect on attitude toward visiting the destination; expectation of visiting the outbound destination has a direct affect on attitude toward visiting the destination and motivation has a mediating effect on the relationship in between expectation and attitude.

What methods can predict future travel behavioural consumption

How to use qualitative of travel behavioural method to predict future travel consumption?

I also suggest to use qualitative of travel behavioural method to predict future travel consumption. Methods such as focus groups interviews and participant observer techniques can be used with quantitative approaches on their own to fill the gaps left by quantitative techniques. These insights have contributed to the development of increasingly sophisticated models to forecast travel behavior and predict changes in behavior in response to change in the transportation system. First, survey methods restrict not only the question frame but the answer frame as well, anticipating the important issues and questions and the responses. However, these surveys methods are not well suited to exploratory areas of research where issues remain unidentified and the researched seek to answer the question "why?". Second, data collection methods using traditional travel diaries or telephone recruitment can under represent certain segments of the population, particularly the older persons with little education, minorities and the poor. Before the survey, focus group for example can be used to identify what socio-demographic variables to include in the survey, how best to structure the diary, even what incentives will be most effective in increasing the response rate. After the survey, focus, focus groups can be used to build explanations for the survey results to identify the "why" of the results as well as the implications. One Asia Pacific survey research result was made by tourism market investigation before. It indicated the travel in Asia Pacific market in the past, had often been undertaken in large groups through leisure package sold in bulk, or in large organized business groups, future travelers will be in smaller groups or alone, and for a much wider range of reasons. Significant new traveler segments, such as female business traveler. The small business traveler and the senior traveler, all of which have different aspirations and requirements from the travel experience.

Moreover, Asia tourism market will start to exist behaviors

in the adoption of newer technologies, a giving the traveler new ways to manage the travel experience, creating new behaviors. This with provide new opportunities for travel providers. The use of mobile devices, smartphones, tablets etc. and social media are the obvious findings to become an integral part of the travel experience. Thus, quality method can attempt to predict Asia Pacific tourism market development in the future.

However, improving the predictive power of travel behavior models and to increase understanding travel behavior which lies in the use of panel data(repeated measures from the same individuals). Whereas, cross-sectional data only reveal inter-individual differences at one moment in time, panel data can reveal intra-individual changes over time. In effect, panel data are generally better suited to understand and predict (changes in) travel behavior. However, a substantial proportion was also observed to transition between very different activity/ travel patterns over time, indicating that from one year to the next, many people renegotiated their activity/travel patterns.

How to apply advanced traveler information systems (ATIS) to predict future travelling behaviour?

Nowadays, information can impact on traveler behavior and network performance. For example, when steadily growing levels of vehicle ownership and vehicle miles traveled information has been identified as a potential strategy towards man aging travel demand, optimizing transportation networks and better utilizing available capacity. Toward, this goal to predict further tourist behavioral consumption. Many countries, government tourism development institutes has applied advanced traveler information systems (ATIS) which travel behavior models and high-fidelity network performance models made increasingly feasible through the rapid advances in computer power. Crucial components of this problem domain are the modeling of individual tourist drivers' response to travel information and the development accurate guidance of relevance to real would trip makers. So, this advanced traveler information systems (ATIS) can assist the tourist who like to rent travelling car tools to travel in any countries own free traveler information systems service conveniently. Also, this travel information system can be intended to assist travelers to make better travel choices. e.g. this system can improve the decision making of individual traveler rather than improvements of network performance overall. So, we need to understand how tourists make their travel plans. Also, understanding decision process that lead to booking of the trip is equally important, as it allows of a potential behavior.

How does online tourism sale channel can influence traveling consumption of behaviour?

Nowadays, internet is popular, it seems that booking air ticket behavior of using internet is predicted to influence overall tourism air tickets payment method. Tourism industry has grown in the previous several decades. Despite its global impact, questions related to better understanding of tourists and whose habits. Using online travel air ticket booking benefits include booking electronic air tickets can be made from entering any electronic travel agents websites in the short time and electronic travel ticket payers do not need leave home, who can pay visa card to pre booking any electronic travel ticket from online channel conveniently.

How to analyze activity based travel demand ? Nowadays, human are concerning the traffic congestion and air quality deterioration, the supply oriented focus of transportation planning has expanded to include how to manage travel demand within the available transportation supply. Consequently, there has been an increasing interest in travel demand management strategies, such as congestion pricing that attempts to change aggregate travel demand. The prediction aggregate level, long term travel demand to understanding disaggregate level (i.e. individual levels) behavioral responses to short term demand policies, such as ride sharing incentives, congestion pricing and employer based demand management schemes, alternate work schedules, telecommuting limitation of travel agent traditionally work nature shall influence oriented trip based travel modelling passenger travel demand indirectly.

Finally, online travel purchase will be popular to influence the number of travel behavioural consumption nowadays. Any travel package products can be sold from websites to attract travellers to choose to prebook air ticket for any trips conveniently. In the past ten years, the internet has become the predominant carrier of all types of information and transactions. Regarding travel decisions, internet has also become an important sales channels for the travel industry, because it is associated with comparably lower distribution and sales costs, but also because ir adapts to hign supply and demand dynamics in this industry. Consequently, the travel and tourism industry tries to increase the internet sale specific share of sales volumes. So, internet sale channel has changed travel consumption behavioural pattern and characteristics and travel experience. For example, Switzerland has one of the highest population-to-computer ratio in Europe. It is also one of the most highly internet penetrated countries in terms of use of the WWW on a day-to-day basis, with more than 75 percent of the population older than 14 years using the WWW daily (ICT, 2005).

The reason of booking online tourism may include: convenience, fast transaction, finding traveling package choice easily, more airline seats available. So, online booking tourism will influence the traditional tourism agents visiting of sales and air tickets and travelling package numbers to be decreased. Finally, the online booking tourism market shares will be expanded to more than traditional tourism agents visits sale market in the future one day. So, the travel agents who still use the traditional tourism visiting sale channel which ought raise whose features to compare to differ to online tourism sale channel if these traditional touriam agents want to keep competitive ability in tourism industry for long term.

Actively based patterns of urban population of travel behavioural prediction method.

Actively based patterns of urban population. It is a method of motivational framework means in which societal constraints and inherent individual motivations interact to shape activity participation patterns. It can be used to predict one city or urban the numbers of travel demand in the year. It has two elements: First, capability constraints refer to constraints are imposed by biological needs, such as eating and sleeping and/or resources, such as income, availability of cars etc. to undertake the urban or city's family activities in the year. Second, coupling constraints define where, when and the duration of planning activities that are to be pursued with other individuals. So, this method needs to gather information (data) to get the relationship between activities, travel and spending work time and space time to evaluate whether there are how many families who have real needs to spend time to go to travel in the year.

What is trip based versus activity based approaches?

What is trip based versus activity based approaches? The fundamental difference between the trip-based and activity based approaches is that the former approach directly focuses on trips without explicit recognition of the motivation or reason for the trips and travel. The activity based approach , on the other hand, views travel as a demand derived from the need to pursue travel activities. So, it is better understand the individual or family behavior basis for individual or family travelling decision regarding participation in travelling activities in certain places or cities or countries at given times and hence the resulting travel needs. This behavioral basis includes all the factors that influence the why, how, when and where of performed activities and resulting individuals and household, the cultural/social norms of the community and the travel surrounding environment.

Another difference between the two approaches is in the way travel is represented. The trip based approach represents travel as a collection of trips. Each trip is considered as independent of other trips, without considering the inter-relationship in the choice attributes , such as time, destination and mode of different trips. As tours are chains of trips beginning and ending at a same location , say home or work. The tour based representation helps maintain the consistency across and capture the interdependency and consistency of the modeled choice attributed among the trips of the same tour.

In addition to the tour based representation of travel, the activity based approach focuses on sequences or patterns of activity participation and travel behavior, using the whole day or longer periods of time is the unit of analysis. Such as approach can address travel demand management issues through an examination of how people modify their activity participation, for example, will individuals substitute more out-of-home activities for in home activities in the evening of who arrived early form work due-to a work schedule change?

The major difference between trip based and the activity based approaches is in the way, the time dimension of activities and travel is considered. In the trip based approach, time is reduced to being simply a cost making a trip and a day's viewed as a combination, defined peak and off peak time periods. On the other hand, activity based approach views individuals' activity travel patterns are a result of their time use decisions with a continuous time domain. As individuals have 24 hours in a day or multiples of 24 hours for longer periods of time and decide how to use that travel among or allocate that time to activities and travel and with who, subject to their socio-demographic, transportation system and other and scheduling of trips. So, determining the impact of travel demand management policies on time use behavior is an important step to assessing the impact of such policies on individual travel behavior. The final major difference between this two approaches relates to the level of aggregation. In the trip based approach, most aspect of travel, e.g. number of trips etc. are analyzed at an aggregate level.

Consequently, trip based methods accommodate the effect of socio-demographic attributes of households and individuals in a very limited fashion, which limits the activity of the method to evaluate travel impacts of long term socio-demographic characteristics of the individuals who actually make the activity travel choices and the travel service characteristics of the surrounding environment. So, the activity based models are better equipped to forecast the longer term changes in travel demand in response composition and the travel environment of urban areas. Also, using activity based models, the impact of policies can be assessed by predicting individual level behavioral responses instead of employing trip based statistical averages that are aggregated over defined demographic segments.

Why senior age will be main travelling target?

In the past, Germany government had established tourism survey analysis to analyze survey data in order to arrive at reliable conclusions on future trends in travel behavior. To aim to find how demographic change will influence the tourism market and how the industry can adapt to those changes. The travel analysis provided data on tourism consumer behavior, including attitudes, motives and intentions. Since, 1970 year, it is based on a random sample, representative for the population in private households aged 14 years or older. Then, a continuous high scientific standard combined with a national and international users makes the travel analysis a useful tool and reliable source for tourism industry and policy decisions. It aimed to gather statistical data. e.g. on the age structure and on demographic trends, quantitative and qualitative analysis with time series data from the travel analysis. It shows e.g. not only the future volume , quite different from today's seniors, or how who will travel of family holidays will change, e.g. single parents of low, but grandparents of growing significance for tourism.

Demographic change is said to be one of the important drivers for new trends in consumer traveling change behavior in most European countries (e.g. Lind 2001). Because the growing number of senior citizens in the European Union and other industralised countries, such as the USA and Japan, looks to become one of the major marketing challenges for the tourism industry. United Nations statistics predict that the share of people being 60 age or older will grow dramatically in the coming future, and is expected to rise from 10 percent of the world population in 2000 year to more than 20 percent in 2050 year (United Nations Population Division, 2001). From its statistic, some data showed that travel propensity increased throughout life until the age of about 50 years of age and was then kept stable until very late in life 75 age. The most important results is that the travel propensity when getting older is not going down between 65 and 75 age of course, the overall development of this variable is influenced by a lot of other factors which are rsponsible for quite a variation over time. It is now possible to suggest that the general pattern of travel propensity is one of the key indicators for holiday life cycle travel behaviour, includes three stages. The growth stage tends to increase from early aduithood until 45 age old or when reaching some 80%. The next stage is stabilisation from the ages of around 50 age,until 75 age old, starting with a lower increase. Finally, the decrease stage is a slight decrease occurs once people reach the more advanced age of 75 age to 85 age old (Lohmann & Danielsson 2001).

So, it seems Germany government tourism prediction to future travellers' behaviour indicated these findings, such as on how future senior generations will travel, who had used survey data to examine the patterns of travel behaviour of a generation getting older and applied the findings to draw conclusions on the future. Also, it predicted that on the future of family trips, family semgmentation will be the travel behaviour patterns in the future. These findings together with the statistical data on demographic change allowed for a better understanding of the coming tends in family holidays. It's aim developed in consumer behaviour related to demographic change and predicted what will happen future of tourism one had to consider other influences and drivers as well, for example, trends on the supply side. e.g. low cost airlines or in travelling consumption behaviour in general whether how the past may provide a key to predict travel patterns of senior sitizens to the future.

Given the projected growth of the senior citizens market, designing specific marketing strategies to meet the prospective needs of elderly tourists will become increasingly important. It has been an implict assumption that it will be a close relationship between the travel behaviour of today's senior citizens and the those of future ones. The growing number of senior citizens in the world. e.g. China, Hong Kong, Japan, USA etc. countries. Global senior citizen tourism market will be based solely on demographic predictions about the future of the population's age structure. However, many of these seniors won't only live longer but will be fitter and more active until later in life. Many of the will also have plenty in life. Many of them will also have plenty of time and money to spend on travel. So, will these new seniors behave like today's senior citizens? Will they adopt the same travel behaviour as the previous generation or become a new market of oldies for the leisure and tourism indudtry?

However, to determine the actual number of senior citizens who will be travelling and to sought to evaluate and specify certain difficult to predict the actual numbers of senior citizen to any country. However, they can be based on the implicit assumption that there is a close relationship between the travel behaviour of past, present and future seniors. But is this a valid assumption? As the reiseanalyse travel analysis survey, which was conducted in Germany every year, offered some interesting data possibiltieis. It was designed to monitor the holiday travel behaviour, opinions and attitudes of Germans and has been carried out since 1970 year, questions in the questionnaire. Data are based on face to face interviews, with a representative sample of more than 7,500 repondents, the interviews being carried out in January each year. All results refer to the average for the defined generated, which ranges generally over ten years. The group of people then at the age of 60 to 69 age is described. This corresponds to the same generation ten years ago, when they had an age of 50 to 59 age. When this methodological approach is not necessarily very sophisticated, it does have the important advantages of being cost effective.

Psychological method to predict travel behavioural consumption.

On the psychological view point, I think individual traveler's character will have those kind of personal characteristics. First, simplicity searchers value above everything ease not transparency in their travel planning and holiday making, and are willing to avoid having to go through extensive research. Second, cultural purists use their travel as an opportunity to immerse themselves in an unfamiliar looking to break themselves entirely from their home lives and engage. Sincerely with a different way of living. Third, social capital seekers understand that to be well travelled is a personal quality, and their choices are shaped by their desire to take maximum of social reward from their travel. They will exploit the potential of digital media to enrich and inform their experiences, and structure their adventures always keeping in mind they are being watched by online audiences. Finally, reward hunters seek a return on the investment who make in their busy , high-achieving lives. Linked in part to the growing trend of wellness, including both physical and mental self improvement who seek truly extraordinary and often indulgent or luxurious' must have experiences.

Why needs to know the personal character of individual traveler's characteristics? Because if travel agents could feel which kinds of individual traveler's character, then who can predict which kind of travel package to design to them more easily. For example, how to determine future travel behaviour from past travel experience and perceptions of risk and safety? We need to concern that the influences of past international travel experience, types of risk associated with international travel and the overall degree of safety feeling during international travel on individual's travelling experiences likelihood of travelling to various geographic regions on their next international vacation trip or avoidance of those regions, due to perceived risk. Because individual traveler's experience of safety risk degree to the countries, it will influence who chooses to go to the countries/country to travel again.

Why do travellers avoid certain destinations are as relevant decision making? Why do they choose to go to the country(countries) to travel? Perceptions of risk and safety and travel experiences are likely to influence travel decisions; efforts to predict future travel behaviour can benefit to individual tourist's decision making. As Weber & Bottom (1989) defined risky decision is as "choices among alternatives that can be described by prodability distributions over possible outcomes" (p.114). Some psychologists judge subjective perceptions of physical reality, i.e. image of a particular tourist destination, whereas value judgement refers to the way individual rank destinations according to whose attributes. i.e. attractiveness, safety, risk etc. factors to form on overall image. So, if the individual traveler had unhappy and worried and unsafe experiences to go to where the place(country) to travel during whose vacation time before. Then, this negative travel experience will influence who is afraid to go to the place (country) to travel again. Risk of place, country, destination or region means the danger is relatively high to the place, ie. increasing in airplane accidents, crime or terrorist activity targeting citizens of potential traveler's nationality or the probability of occurrence is great , ie. recent occurrences involving travel regions/destinations under consideration or effective actions to control consequences exist. i.e. selecting safe regions and destinations, taking extra precautions when traveling to risky destinations. These risk factors will influence the individual traveler who chooses to cancel travel plan to go to the country again.

Another interesting research, how to predict behavioural intention of choosing a travel destination, which has focus of toursm research for years, but the complex decision making process leading to the choice of a travel destination has not been well researched. The planned behaviour model using its core constructs, attitude, subjective norm and perceived behavioural control, with the addition of the past behavioural variable on behavioural intention of choosing a travel destination. Understanding why people travel and what factors influence their behavioural intention of choosing a travel destination is beneficial to tourism planning and marketing. Understanding travel motivation is the push and pull model. The idea of the push and pull model is the decomposition of an individual's choice of a travel destination into two forces. The first force is the push factor that pushes an indvidual away home and attempts to develop a general desire to go somewhere else, without specifying where that may be. The second force is the pull factor, that pulls on individual toward a destination, due to a region specific travel location or perceived attractiveness of a destination. The respective push and pull factors illustrate that people travel because who are pushed by their internal motives and pulled by external forces of a destination. Nevertheless, how push and pull factors guide people's attitude and how these attributes lead to behavioural intentions of choosing a travel destination have rarely been investigated. The decision making process leading to the choice of a travel destination is a very complex process. The planned behaviour model is as a research framework to predict the behavioural intention of choosing a travel destination. The model based on the three constructs of attitude, subjective norm, and perceived behavioural control (Fishbein & Ajzen, 1975).

In conclusion, the factors can influence travelers who decide to choose to travel the country, which include personal safety was perceived to the highest motivation factors among the important factors which include, scenic beauty, cultural interests, friendliness of local people, price of trip, services in hotels and restaurants, quality and variety of food and shopping facilities and services. The factors include both push and pull. Push factors include knowledge, prestige, and enhancement of human relationship etc., whereas, the most significant pull factors include high technologic image, expenditure and accessibility etc. For example, Japanese travelers visiting Hong Kong. Push factors are such as exploration dream fulfillment and pull factors are such as benefits sought, attractions and good climate city. It will be the factor of future travel patterns and motivations of sub-cultural and ethic groups for Japanese choice to go to Hong Kong travelling.

Bibliography

Backman, K., Backman, S., Uysal, M. And Sunshine, K. (1995). Event Tourism : An Examination Of Motivations And Activities. Festival Management And Event Tourism, 3(1), 15-24.

Fishbein, M., & Ajzen, Z. (1975). Belief, Attitude, Intention And Behaviour: An Introduction To Theory And Research, Boston: Addison Wesley.

Hsu, C.H.C., Cai , L.A., Li, M(2010). Expectation, Motivation And Attitude: A Tourist Behavioral Model. Journal Of Travel Research, 49(3), 282-296. http://dx.doi, org/10.1177/004728750 9349266.

ICT Information And Communication Technology Switzerland, 2005. ICT Fakten (ICT facts). Available from http://www.ictswitzerland.ch/de/ ict%2fakten/factsfigures.asp(retrieved Dec.12, 2005) in German.

Lind, (2001): Befolkningen, Familjen, Livscykeln- Och

Ekonomisk Tillvaxt. Institutet For Tillvaxtpo-litiska studier/Vinnova/Nutek.

Lohmann, Martin (2001): The 31 st. Reiseanalyse-RA 2001. Tourism: vol. 49, no.1/2001;pp.65-67, Zagreb.

United Nations Population Division (2001). World Population Prospects: The 2000 year Revision, New York.

Weber E.U., & W, P.Bottom (1989). "Axiomatic Measures Of Perceived Risk: Some Tests And extensions." journal of behavioral decision making, 2 (2): 113-31.

Online travel agent and offline travel agent strategy

The difference between online and offline travel agents

The main cost related factors to offline or online travel agents

Nowadays,many online or offline travel agents have interest to find what the main factors that can affect their strategies to reduce airline costs. The main factors include route structure, type and characteristics of the aircracft, cost of labor and management quality, which will influence whether which airline routes are the most suitable to let online travel agents or offline travel agents to help them to sell paper air tickets or electronic air tickets to attract travel consumption more easily.

Thus, a cost-related strategy is the main important factors to influence travel consumption choice between online or offline travel agents. For example, considering that advantages in costs is an important strategy for carriers to remain in travel transportation market.

The deregulation process of travel markets and increasing opportunities for competition have created excess capacity in many markets that causes lower rates, even with its rising costs. Thus, the travel strategic costs management as well as travel consumers that their behavior under different influences can bring competitive advantages over travel players.

Cost reduction in the travel market -based industry is a very important way of being competitive between offline and online travel agents, when facing travel air ticket prices decreasing for every trip. So reduce to total travel cost, e.g. fuel, maintenance, labor etc. is relevant, but the influence of ech component on every total trip cost depends on factors that are related or not to airline opertion. For example, some airline can adopt the lowest cost model to sell air tickets from offline or online travel agents which compete for travel passengers with traditional modes as self driving road transport trip in large areas of countries domestic travel market, such as US, UK domestic travel market.

However, the decision about the relevance of one cost is not a simple matter. The effectiveness of reduction of each item that comprises the total cost of airline can change over time, depending on both the business model and the scope of the airline company or online /offline travel agent company as well as external factors.

However, there are three types of competition advantage between online and offline travel market: They are such as agility, differentiation cost and the differentiation may be related to a product of superior quality, higher value f the brand or the company's positive reputation. Such as the online travel agent's providing the different airline cheap air ticket price and kind of trips to provide to travel consumer consumer comparison or the offline travel agent's famous brand or positive reputation to let travel consumers feel travel agents can provide many actual trip package to let them to compare by oral clearly. Thus, the online travel agent's weakness is lack of travel agent individual exploration to let every travel consumer to understand every trip package more clearly.

But online travel agent's strength is it can provdide one website to let travel consumer attempt to compare different trip air ticket and/or hotel price to make personal travel pre-booking decision at home. The another advantage is related to techniques that reduce production cost, making it is possible to offer cheaper air ticket, or hotel room rents, or cheap trip package, than the competition. Such as online travel agent can sell more cheape electronic air ticket price to compare traditional offline travel agent's paper air ticket price.

Finally, agility refers to the speed which the company responds to market demands. For example, if the online travel agent can make statistics to analyze how many online travel consumers to choose to buy which airlines' electronic or paper air tickets, e.g. which airline trip destinations and trips and hotels choices are the most popular attraction to them. Then, the online airline has possible to respond to provide to the most popular airline trips choices, electronic air ticket price comparison choices and hotel rooms prices choices to attract many online travel consumers to enter their online travel websites to choose different airline electronic tickets to buy or pre-book hotel rooms from travel agent websits. Also, if the traditional offline travel agents cn attempt to gather every travel consumer's destination trips, hotels , airline paper or electronic ticket prices enquires to make statistics to make which travel trip journeys or destinations and airline paper travel ticket prices are the most popular. Then, it is possible that they can respond to every travel consumer individual demand more to attract whose travel agent choice more easily.

Airline travel agency AirAsia in the domestic airline low cost strategy

There are three major characteristics of the airline industry namely is product nature, its expenditure structure and its market entry conditions. Airline agent's product is homogeneous or undifferentiated , causing significant competition in airline domestic travel or foreign travel both markets, which are free from regulations and economic barriers. However, high capital and operating expenditure is another important characteristic of the airline industry. Aircrafts, airlines' major capital expenditure are very costly to acquire . For operating expenditures, aviation fuel and labor make up the two major costs in the industry.

Another important characteristic of the airline industry is the conditions for market entry, which differs between international and domestic airline markets . In the international travel market, airline travel agency entry is very difficult as international flights and routes are the results of regotiations between governments . On the other hand, in the domestic and regional travel market, travel agency entry depends on the level of deregulation or liberalisation.

More and more countries, however are opening up their domestic travel markets for more competition. In addition, government plays an important role to regulate the travel markets and existing players may significant influence over now travel agent entrants.

In fact, the mjor factors influence to international or domestic travel consumption increasing numbers are the global economy and safety issues, instead of other different economic factors, such as travel destination choice, electronic air ticket or paper air ticket price, hotel price , the country's political change, e.g. war occurrence, bad weather , e.g. very cold or very hot etc. different factors infuence. Because generally , the world or any region of it is in an economic crisis or depression , the demand for airline services will fall. The late 1990 year Asian financial crisis for example, resulted in minimal increase in the number of worldwide airline passengers incrased only minimally from 1997 to 1998 year. Another factor of influencing the travel passenger number to be decreased, it concerns safety issues are also an important driver of the travel industry, which is subject to very safety standards to influence travel passengers' travel choice to the country. In addition, they are also unexpected safety related events, such as the 11 Sept. 2001 year tragedy in the US, which caused reduction in passengers . The increasing popularity of low cost airlines is the newest trend in the airline industry if which hope many passengers choose to buy whose electronic air ticket or paper air ticket to catch which planes to fly from online travel agent or offline travel agent channels.

The rise of low cost airlines, such as AmericaWest, JetBlue and Airtran in US, Ryanair and EasyJet in Europe and Vigin Blue in Australia. The share of low cost airline strategy is popular in the US and European airline market. For example, the Southwest airline low cost strategy is the basis of most low cost airlines operations. The key of the strategy is to reduce costs when at the same time offering low prices to passengers. History showed that the low cost airline strategy is easy to replicate , but difficult to implement successfully.

However, I suggest airlines need to know what functions which can attract passengers to chose to catch their planes to fly if they expect to rise passenger numbers. For example, the critical function of the Malaysia airline travel is to connect the major towns and remote interior areas within East Malaysia, which has poor road systems and limited availability of other significant means of transportation . In constrast, West Malaysia has more developed and extensive rod and railway systems.

Therefore, airline travel is not the main mode of long distance transportation. It implies Malaysis airline ought concentrate on focusing short distance transportation strategy for passenger benefitical choice function. For example, a new small Malaysia airline serving one or two routes may enter easily. Otherwise, a larger airline servicing multiple routes may be harder to enter Malaysia airline market. It also means access to capital and labor are the major obstacles for new airline entrants to Malaysia airline market. Thus, small airlines into a larger airline is probably more likely to be successful as in Air Asia's case to Malaysia airline market.

Thus, the airline low cost strategy competition positions include very low or minimal pressive from other airline similar service substitute products, low or medium power of airline similar input suppliers. In conclusion, low cost airline strategy is a god method to be attempted to win competitors in airline market.

How consumers select travel service between online and offline mode in travel industry

Nowadays, the travel industry is operating through two different modes, online and offline respectively. It involves the identification of the competitive strategies adopted by the tour operators. For example, it was found that e-retil travel is platform that is bringing two market forced the demand and supply tour operators and the customers together, and both parties and more inclined towards online mode in near future. Tour operators are gaining by operating at low cost and increasing their business reach when customers get what they desire as per their convenience. For example, many tour operators had promoted tourism destination through website that allow user to use interface for booking transporttion, foreign exchange etc. However, the role of travel operators (agents) should be assisted any airlines to promote their travel package service by internet more easily , such as tourism destination , arrangement of hospitality, restaurants, transportation tools during their trips.

The reasons why consumers choose online travel service include:

Firstly, it is online researching hospitality service. Online travel websites can provide many different accommodation furnitures, such as seeking hotel locations, rooms prices comparison, prepaid hotel rooms by visa card payment transaction method, range from luxury five stars deluxe ctegory hotels to small guest houses. The primary need of tourist is to find a place for residing in foreign country or domestic country to ensure whose safety and relaxing needs. Online travel website channel can help whom to find a place , according to his/her needs and paying capacity in the most shorten times.

Secondly, it is online restaurant (food and beverages researching) service. Full service restaurants are divided into two categories, fine dining and casual dining restaurants . Fine dining restaurants are usually located in the premises of luxury hotels, provide high quality food at premium price with good ambience and highly trained professionals. Thus, travel consumers can also compare the different restaurant food price and seek where is the restaurant and find.

What food taste of food supply from the travel agency or travel operator website easily 250 + tour operators are registered with the ministry of tourism (website of tourism ministry) , and the major players in the industry are dealing online and are dominating the travel industry. The major online travel players are Thomas cook, Cox and Kings, make any trips, clear trip, gatra.com and Expedia.

The tour operators whether online or offline offers a large number of services to the touists including customized package where the customer selects each element of the tour package, speciallized tourism package and complete tour guide package.

Nowadays, the tour operational travel (agents) are working through two different modes: offline online . Big brands with luge investment are dealing online and enjoying low cost benefits and huge profit margins. When the small tour operators have their market niche and managing have their market niche and managing their profits by dealing offline.

It is generally prefer offline mode that is the opportunity for small capital investment or employee number for tour operators. But the large scenario is changing as with the usage of internet by the tour operations have given convenience to the customers and now the customers of modern age have started developing preference for online modern. Thus, internet technology change any countries' travel agents or tour operators' air ticket sale method. So, it brings electronic ticket sale method is more popular to compare to traditional travel paper air ticket sale method.

However, online electronic ticket sale method has its disadvantages such as online transaction is unsafe, if the consumer 's name and address and visa card number is stolen to let any internet users to know to be used to buy any products from internet channel easily. Otherwise, traditional walk in offline travel paper ticket sale method is more sfe, because the travel consumers can pay cash to the travel agents directly.

However, offline travel agent disadvantages include that the research identified that information communication and technology has very crucial role for tourism industry. Tourist can access any kind of information about tourism destination and tourism products from any part of the world. Tourism comprehends with social media. For example, it was found that (ICT) is bosting up tourism industry. (ICT) helps in searching the location, search for information on tourism products, and e-booking of airline tickets and hotel reservation.

The online travel sale service attraction is that the recent development in the field of informatin communication and technology and its practical application in tourism and hospitality industry. Generally , online travel sale service must have consumer side and the supplier side.

The decision making prcess of consumer was analyzed and it was found that travel information search and traveller individual electronic ticker pre paid to prebook any plane seat, hotel rooms and restaurants prices comparison to prebook service of traveler individual purchase behavior are corresponding with the usae of (ICT).

What is the online travel sale service strategy?

The two most important things for travel operators (agents) are online travel marketing and strategic management. Former can enhance business operations. Use of (ICT) develops financial capabilities , however, it depends on management choice, financial condition and position. Some researchers recommended that the usage of IT should not be restricted at operatinal level, however it should be extended up to senior level and should be used for decision making. Social media is regarded as a platform where the tourists and travel operators/agents (suppliers) of tourism industry cross each other. Thus, the role of social media has been directed for future research in tourism industry. Hence, it seems online travel sale service has these features to attract travel consumers to choose to use this online mode to buy electronic air ticket. Such as, airline electronic air ticket price comparison, pre-booking plan seats to avoid full seats flights to delay consumer individual trip plan, pre-booking hotel rooms and prices comparison as well as prebooking restaurant seats and food price and taste comparison, travel destination easy search. Otherwise, these features to attract travel consumers to choose to walk in to travel agents to buy paper air ticket directly. They include: safe cash or visa card payment to avoid personal information is stolen by website payment channel, e.g. via card number, address, name , birth date personal information. Also the travel consumer can enquire any questions from the travel agent and gets individual feedback from the travel agent by oral before who ensure to choose to buy which kind of travel package for whose travel destination. In special, when the travel consumer has much time to spend to enquire any travel trip question, walk in travel agent is the best enquire methos to let the travel consumer to know the trip information clearly.

● Online/offline travel operators
(agents) maketing strategies

Offline walk in travel unique segment service strategy

Nowadays, online and offlce travel operators competitions are serious. In fact, tourism marketing , there will be more need for online travel operators in the future, due to online travel sale service is popular to be accepted by online travel consumers. Thus, I recommend walk in offline travel agents need to concentrate on focusing some unique travel service to attract new or old travel consumers if who hope to survive.

I recommend that they can focus on specific specialized services, such as travel consultation (specialization) hypothesizing that systematic differences exist between the usage of travel agents for different travel contexts and travel agents can survive if they focus on specific segments of the market, such as older travelers (segmentation; hypothesizing that systematic differences exist between the usage of travel agents depending on the personal characteristics of travellers). The unique travel needs include: specific services related to package holidays, transport services, beach on city holidays, as well as destinations travellers are not familiar with.

I shall give my opinions to provide insight into alternative strategies for travel agencies in a matured travel market with a high internet penetration as below:

The internet online travel sale service is a reality of popular to let travel consumers to feel convenient to pre-book air seat, hotel rooms , air electronic ticket prices comparison. In order to make final purchase decision very easily in the shortest time. Consequently , it has penetrated the decision making process of travel to attract them to choose to buy electronic air ticket, prebooking hotel rooms or restaurant seats from online travel agent channel more than walk in offline travel agent channel. This is especially true in the tousism business where consumption to consume (booking) and the purchase-related information search (Bieger & Lasesser 2004; Crotts 1998).

In fact , apply website to provide travel sale method has these good consequence. From travel operator (agent) supplier's perspective, the success potential derived from operating a website consist of lower distribution costs, higher revenues and a larger potential market share (due to the ubiquitous access). From traverler's perspective, the internet allows direct communication with tourism suppliers facilitatinf requests for information and allowing services and travel related products, e.g. prebooking hotel rooms, restaurant seats , electronic or paper air tickets, travel trip arrangement package products to be purchased at any time and any place from online travel agents /operators conveniently.

Offline / online travel agency (operator) business depends on earn commissions on behalf of airlines. Thus, offline walk in travel agency (operator) business model that would extend existence as a booking agency (thus focusing on consultation and interpersonal contact) strategy.

As a matter of fact, commission -cutting , which began in the US well ahed of Europe, has had a profound effect specially on business travel agents . Consequently , many of them have re-invented themselves as " travel managers", instead of selling tickets and making arrangements, they charge consultancy fees for reducing the amounts client companies spend on travel (Daneshku, 1999).

Systematic differences strategy applies to offline walk in travel agent

Thus, I recommend systematic differences strategy can be

applied offline walk in travel agent (operator). It means that walk in travel agents could reorient their offline walk in travel agent business to focus on contexts that are less substitutable by other channels and media . Factors hypothetically attributing to the delineation of travel contexts include: helping travellers to choose best travel destinations, helping travellers to attempt to find the number of previous trips (indicating the familiarity with a destination) for their travel reference, helping them to find the cheapest, the most convenient and the most close transportation to ctch during their trips, helping them to find the different types of accommodation and rooms price comparison , nature/type of the trip comparison , arrangement of time of booking (as indicator of spontneous / planned travel) nd helping them to budget overall travel expenditure .

Systematic differences in travel agent use exist in dependence of personal (characteristics with with tourists. Walk in offline travel agents could benefit from a travelling client segmentation strategy and customize and target their services to those travellers that are most likely to be and remain their customers.

Factors hypotheticlly attributing to the traveller segment include: travel expenditure per day, useful travel information as indicator for perceived risk and socio-demographic (age, gender, highest completed and education, professional positions) . Generally, the role of walk in offline travel agent with regard to the travel infrormation search and booking behavior have take an incoming perspective. Such as looking at visitors from different travel markets at a similar destinations. The comparison of central importance in determining whether specialization of travel contexts or market segments is the more promising strategy for walk in offline travel agents. However, travel package tours strategy must b offline walk in travel attraction . Due to some walk in travellers target segmentation market has still needs. Generally, this travel package tours of travel segmentation consumer who like to enquire the travel agents to concern what the hotel rooms price are the cheapest to provide to them to live, what transportation tools the travel agent can arrange to them to catch anywhere the country destination, the travel agent can provide them to visit during their tour journey. Thus, the travel trip package service is still popular need to offline walk in travel agent (operator). This market is only belonged to offline walk in travel agents (operators) nowadays.

Service fees and commission cuts strategy

The reduction or removal of airline commission continues to challenge travel agencies' profitabilityl It is crucial to understand what trends travel agencies need to be aware of to ensure how to optmse profitability and increase travel agencies' revenues with service-fee models. Service fees are not only a way to compensate for the loss of airline commission but also a way to generate new revenue sources for travel agencies that guarantee their long term profitability. Many travel agencies are expanding their service fee models, both in terms of the mounts changed and the number of service to airline.

However, if travel agent charge too much service fee to exceed the general airline travel market service fee reasonable or standard level. It will influence many airlines do not choose to find the travel agent to help them to sell air tickets. Travel agents apply fees most often for airline related services. They charge differentiated fees depending on the destination, type of reservation (e.g. frequent flyer), number of tickets sold or type of airline (e.g. full service versus).

However, service fee increaes can raise customer loyalty and satisfaction. It won't reduce client numbers or result ina losee in clients.. The reason is that service fees can be tailored to suit individual customer. Ths helps travel agencies target their clients, with tailored services based on their past purchasing patterns and identity services for which clients' willingness to pay is greater , such as trip planning identity service for which pay , such as hotel only or special promotion.

To revenue mix for travel agencies is increasingly shifting to service fes as airlines have lowered or cut commissions. Successful travel agencies in many European countries are fast adopting, and constantly upgrading , their service fee schemes. Thus, it seems reasonable service fee level is one important factor to influence travel agents and airlines good relationship. In fact, even travel agents raise service fee, it won't influence travel consumer number to be reduced , even they raise air ticket price. It they can provide the informations concerning the reasonable hotel roomes prices and food quality comparison to satisfy travel consumers' living arrangement or helping them to find the reasonable restaurants' food prices and where are their location arrangement or providing the reasonable airlines' electronic air tickets or paper air tickets sale service, even arrangement any high entertainment quality of travel destination trips to let travel consumers to feel satisfactory. However, I believe the raise air ticket price factor won't inffluence the travel consumer number to be decreased. Any offline or online travel agents will encounter this crisis. By cutting travel agents' commission. Airlines decreased their dependence on travel agencies as a distribution channel. In fact, three key variable factors will influence travel agents' commission income to be decreased. They include below:

● The unsustainable or no change financial losses by airlines , due to the growth of low cost carriers, leading to an increase in the number of bankruptcies.

● No negative consequences from previous commission cuts: airline had progressively lowed the commission payments.

● No effective resource for travel agencies to satisfy airlines needs.

● The appearance of now airlines and air routes to provide to travel agencies to fall down air ticket price to attract consumers' choices, due to who don't feel to spend much money to go to this new air routes or catch new airline plans , whether these new air routes are excite to entertainment or whether they are safe planes to catch.

● An increase in the number of bankruptcies to cause travel comsumption desire to be reduced.

● New competition forced down air fares.

● The necessity to cut production costs, especially with low cost meaning low production costs and low fares, even if the two are closely linked.

Internet negative influences to travel agents

Although, on the one hand, internet creates offline travel agents to use websites to help them to sell electronic air ticket or travel related products, such as prebooking hotel rooms , restaurants, transportation tools etc. travel service. However, on the other hand, internet also brings travel agencies competitive disadvantage with regad to suppliers' direct websites , when airlines are able to control seat availability and prices. Indeed internet cause the decision is made by the airlines to reduce and/or eliminate travel agency commission has led them to use technology that many of their distrust or are not inclined to use, and to compare prices and travel schedules constantly.

As a result of this travel sale service environment, traditional offline travel agencies are at a competitive disadvantage with regard to online travel agencie and to airline carriers, which have developed their own direct websites where they are able to control seat availability and prices.

Nevertheless, travel agents' pay programmes remain. From some airlines, travel agents receive negotiated incentive commission closely linked to their performance as incentive . However, airlines still need travel agents' assistance to help them to promote air tickets to sell, due to travel agents can provide trip packages, transportation tools, prebooking hotel rooms, restaurants and air tickets arrangement and they can give any enquiries to every individual travel consumer. It is free charge travel professional enquiry service for travel agency's competitive features.

Consequently, how agencies can reduce their reliance on airline commission payments. I recommend these following strategic options to them to apply as below:

● Streamlining operations, controlling staff costs, when ensuring the client feels as little impact as possible.

● Expanding or moving into the leisure business, where commissions on ono-air products remain high (cruise, hotel, railway travel)

● Specializing in geographic areas or becoming niche players for specific leisure products, e.g. destination weddings, student travel group cultural travel, cruises only, cruise and railway travel etc.

● (d) establishing a service fee driven business model.

Concentrating on business travel marketing strategy

The certain characteristics to the business travel market allowed this sector to adapt more easily to the disappearance of commission. Business travel systems have always had different relationship with different customers. They usually have long term buyer relationships, set up long before the commission cap. Some of them quickly renegotiated their contracts to include a transaction or management fee, knowing that the majority of these fee arrangements are specific the need of the client.

The reasons why airlines reduce commission to paid to travel agents. They include petrol costs increasing, e.g. indirect and by pass the established distribution chain by developing airlines' their own websites; reducing or removing commission paid to travel agencies. Consequently, the decision to cut travel agencies' commission clearly shows that airlines wanted to decrease their reliance and dependence on travel agencies as a distribution channel. Thus, the internet appears to be an efficient and cost-effective distribution channel. Also, by creating airlines' own websites and setting directly to their clients, airlines are also to control seat availability to their clients and prices to their websites.

What an e-commerce strategy is used by internet travel websites?

Nowadays, the commercial use of electronic travel ticket travel is common, the most purchased online products include, for example, the name brands in online travel Epedia.travel .com and cheap tickets have been or are being integrated in large online travel firms.

Generally, online travel websites apply these strategies to attract travel consumers as below:

Firstly, shopping mall strategy, means to conduct a comprehensive factors for e-commerce. The online service provider needs to organize catalogs of services, take orders through their websites, accept payments securely, send service or related document, such as airline tickets to consumers and manage client data , such as client profiles.

Secondly, portal strategy, portal websites , such as yahoo give visitors the chance to find almost everything , they are working for in one place. Websites , such as Altavista.com and yahoo.com provide users with a shopping page that links them to many sites carrying a variety of products. Once a client is familiar with a website, who will be more likely to use the online service.

Thirdly, pricing strategy, low price is as a major competitive weapon. It includes a comparison pricing on discount price or price negotiation to let online travel consumers to get the best electronic travel ticket price choice to buy any airline tickets.

Travel agents vs online booking: Tackling the shortcomings and strengths

Consequently, however, one travel consumer who chooses either online booking sale service or traditional walk in offline travel agent to enquire travel service. These both of travel sale methods have shortcomings also. Such as it is possible that online electronic travel ticket purchase has personal data ,e.g. visa card, name, birth data, address, which will be stolen by online crime internet users more easily, who can not enquire any travel questions to get clear travel information concern whose travel destination package service choice or hotel room choice or transportation tool or restaurant choice and airline choice by travel agent. Also, it is possible that walk in travel agent paper travel ticket purchase shortcomings include that the travel consumer can not check any airlines' seat and pre book hotel room or transport tool or restaurant in the shorten time if who needs to fly immediately. Thus, it seems that online travel agent's client group is business travel intention, who does not need to enquire travel agent and has desire to per book airline seat in the short time. Otherwise, the offline walk in agent's client group is entertainment intention , who need to walk in to travel agent to enquire whose travel package and has no desire to pre book airline seat in the short time. Thus, online travel agent ought concentrate on design good travel package for the business travel consumers. Otherwise, offline travel agent ought concentrate on design good travel package for the entertainment travel consumers. Thus, they can have themselves unique travel target package to adopt to their different travel need. Such as business travel consumers need to live cheap and comfortable hotels, catching cheap and fast transportation tools in their business trips, eating in cheap and good taste food in restaurant and spending the less time to catch the airline plan to arrive the destination and cheap and comfortable business class plan seat. Such as entertainment travel consumers need the travel agent can help them to design cheap and enjoyable travel package, includes living comfortable hotel room, exciting and enjoyable trip, good taste food and

railway, travel bus, cruise and plane provision in trip.

In conclusion, In fact, tourism is a quite unique area of business in a sense that is a travel sale service product and it can't be observed or manipulated through direct experience prior to purchase . Instead clients have to purely rely on indirect or virtual experience. Thus, every online or offline travel agent ought attempt to design different travel package to attract every business traveler or entertainment traveller trip need because every traveler will have personal unique trip need in this competitive travel sale service market in the future.

4.18 (AI) tool technical innovation in cruise tourism immediate positive emotion influence to cruise travelling consumers

Can apply (AI) tool to cause positive emotion to cruise tourism consumers? Cruise tourism industry is the most influential emotion industry example to influence cruise travelling consumers' travelling entertainment choice. I shall indicate some evidences how it's innovation will influence cruise travelling consumers' emotion to be changed to positive from negative immediately as well as to prove how the cruise traveler higher utility feeling to the cruise tourism provider is not the main factor to influence whom to choose the cruise provider to consume whose cruise journey service arrangement.

Nowadays, cruising has become one of the fastest growing sectors within tourism, cruise service providers need have themselves unique different entertainment service arrangement to satisfy every cruise travelling consumer individual needs in order to attract every one to choose whose cruise arrangement easily, e.g. meals, activities, entertainment and varied destinations create one-stop holiday shop, reasonable competitive ticket fare. Hence, it seems it is one exciting emotion industry. If the cruise service provider can bring positive emotion to influence many cruise travelling consumers immediately. The, even it change higher service fare to compare other similar cruise service providers. I believe it won't influence them to choose other similar cruise service providers if it can often bring immediate positive emotion to its cruise clients during they are staying in its cruises or during they have left its cruises, but they will often remember or won't forget to enjoy their cruise service provider's happing time forever. Hence, if (AI) tool can be attempted to help cruise entertainment providers to arrange different cruise journeys for varied destinations , to arrange different entertainment facilities, to arrange the different taste food to satisfy different countries age cruise consumers' needs. Then, the (AI) tool will assist the cruise providers to bring positive emotion to let every different countries age cruise consumers to feel satisfactory in order to choose to the cruise providers' cruise entertainment service more attractively.

How can apply (AI) tool to predict cruise service providers bring positive emotion to their clients?

Future, (AI) tool can help any cruise providers to design these kinds of any one entertainment service arrangement to satisfy the cruise provider's customers' needs.

There are different special interests cruising , such as wellness at sea, freighter cruises, river cruises. It has increased the attractiveness of cruising: Romance is for lover cruise traveler target, luxury is for rich cruise traveler target, exotica is for enjoyment exciting feeling traveler target. So, every kind of cruise traveler target will have different kind of cruise entertainment service to satisfy their needs. If the cruise service provider can provide the right and attractive cruise entertainment service to satisfy the specific cruise target. Then, it will bring the positive emotion to the specific cruise target consumers more easily.

Cruise travel was shaped for mass tourism. Prices have been very differently segmented. There are basically four types of markets (Biederman, 2008):

● Contemporary market: On board fun and amenities are playing important role and destinations have secondary importance.

● Premium market: This category is more expensive than the contemporary category and where the destination has same importance as on board amenities.

● Luxury market: It was once dominant type of cruise tourism, but now it has only a small portion of the industry. Generally, it is the most expensive cruise category and usually it takes longer than average cruise days.

● Adventure/exploration: It refers relatively long cruises with special and exotic places where the destination is the main purpose of the trip.

● European cruise travel: Duration takes more five days than worth American travel duration. There is a tendency on European market during the years that duration of travel is getting shorter. This short demand of is explained with the strong demand of customers (Hensen, 2003). Beside this, it is most likely that cruise companies try to convince tourists with short haul travels instead of long term cruise trips for more expenditure.

Thus, I believe that even, the cruise service provider charges higher ticket which won't influence cruise consumers who do not choose its entertainment service on its cruises. If it can arrange the attractive cruise entertainment facilities and destination journey arrangement, staying days arrangement to satisfy different specific cruise target market needs absolutely in order to bring whose emotion to be positive to it's service provision.

Then, the cruise service provider will attract many potential cruise clients to choose its cruise service absolutely. Otherwise, if it only bring negative emotion to its cruise clients, it will not attract many potential cruise clients to choose it or loses its old cruise clients, even, its cruise ticket price is needed to decreased in order to raise competitive effort.

In conclusion, I believe that future (AI) tools need to learn how to bring cruise consumers to arise individual immediate or expected positive emotion, this positive emotion consideration is more important to compare to how to reduce cruise ticket price in order to attract cruise clients in global cruise competitive cruise industry.

Differentiation through the characteristi of cruising route method from (AI) tool route judgement

Future, (AI) tool can attempt to help any cruise entertainment service providers to judge how to design different route to attract different countries age cruise clients' choices to satisfy their cruise journey entertainment needs. The determinants of the cruising route's characteristics (functional, social, and emotion) is important factor to influence the cruise service provider's success. Cruising product is no longer selected primarily for the cruising service, but for the content of cruising route. So, the cruising route will influence the cruise consumer individual emotion, because it is the main service need for every cruise consumer.

The approach called the " land sea cruising in product development" is increasingly becoming an area of interest, e.g. determining the direction of the effects of the individual cruising route characteristics on service value's perception , and providing an evaluation model of the route's perception , and indicating significance variables of attraction.

The questions that cruise planners need to know: How does each of the identified determinants affect the overall perceived value of the cruise route? How the overall perceived value of the cruise route affects customer behavior intentions?

Because different routes factor will influence cruise consumer individual emotion changing seriously. It means the ship has become only a tool, when the offered route whose attractiveness highly influences the impression of the guests has become crucial.

Consumer behavior in cruising segment includes all the activities and influences in the selection of the specific cruise route. There activities result in decisions and actions related to a defined price, selection and reselection of cruising company (Cannot, Brink and Brijball, 2006).

How to apply (AI) tool to arrange cruise route planning have close relationship to influence cruise consumer emotion?

Firstly, use value of cruising routes is based on the subjective experience, and shows how individuals assess the route during, or immediately after sailing. It is affiliated with the benefits that cruising guest realize by choosing a route , and it is subjective because it depends on the individual assessment (photo taken on the route for one guest presents just a family souvenir, and for professional photographers are embodied financial capital).

Secondly, the utilitarian value is also subjective-oriented and is tied on the point where the inner and us ability of cruising routes are compared with the sacrifice of the client (money and time). Finally, the value is considered as the outcome of the comparison of scarifies and personal benefits, which is resulted in essentially utilitarian nature.

Hence, route design is the main value of cruising tourism and it is primarily determined and analyzed from the aspect of observed customers. Otherwise, the cruise is only one tool to be caught for the cruise passengers, whether the cruise can let whom to sleep comfortable , providing what kind of food to them to eat, what kind of entertainment facilities are provided to them to play, these issues are not more important to compare how to design route to bring them to travel to anywhere to enjoy in this cruise journey factor. Because how to design the route factor can bring each cruise passenger to influence them to feel either negative or positive emotion directly. The whole route journey planning is the most influential factor to influence the cruise passengers to feel whether they ought choose it's service again or not in the future.

Reference

Bieger. Th., and Ch. Laesser (2004). " Information sources for travel decisions: Toward a source process model," Journal of travel reserch, 42(4): 357-371.

Daneshku, S. (1999). " Unwived travel agents unworried bi internet, " Financial Times , London. June 16, 1999:10.

Foucault, B. Lery, N. Rifkin, A. & Silfies , 2000.
" Comparision of textbook prices by retailer and by college" working paper. Cornell University, Ithaca, Ney.

CHAPTER V

How social change influence human leisure need change

Human Behavioral network job brings social economic benefits

What does human network job mean ? Why may human network job be popular? Why human network job behavior may influence economy ?

Nowadays internet is popular to use. We can apply internet to find data , search any new things, even earn money. Why does internet

may become huma network job source. For example, e-publish may be one kind of new human network job. Any authors may apply internet

channel to help them to sell electronic or paper books from e-publisher web store. They may apply facebook, you tub etc. any online

channel to promote themselves new books to let new readers to know whether when they may buy themselves favourable new topic books to read

from electronic publisher web store.

Thus, future electronic publisher industry may help any authors to build internet network platform to help them to sell and promote

ot advertise their any one new electronic or paper book topic to let global any one reader to choose to buy their any new topic books from electronic publisher web store easily and conveniently. However, it implies that electronic network platform author may be one kind of future new human network job in our societies.

How electronic network platform author job may bring economy benefit in macro economy view? A person can have few friends, contacts and still be very influential if these few
friends and contacts are themselves highly influential, e.g. one author must not need to know any one reader in global society. When they like to choose any electronic books from electronic internet network platform. They may become the author's any one topic book buyer, when they feel the author's any one topic book is fun and attract they make decision to buth the strange author whose the topic book from electronic book publisher's platform web store conventiently in short time. Although, they are strangers, they do not know themselves , but the reader can understand what it way that made Google from writing platofrm to create new creative mind and typing network job method to replace traditional hand writing book method for global authors. It will be one kind of new human network writing job.

Hence, global any one reader can apply an innovative search engine , such as google.com to find whether whom author personal new topic books are value to read from internet.
Then, the electroniuc publisher's web store may be new book store platform sale network to help the author to sell many electronic or paper books from electronic network platform
in short time. So, internet may be future new network plaform to help global any one author to create network writing job absolutely. Furthermore, internet may be

popular social media

to help any one author to build goold relationship between his/her readers. It is one kind of new network, human network job. New authors do not need to buy many paper books to prepare to put in any one book shop warehouse. Their every book can print on demand to reduce out of book stock in any one book shop. They may choose to sell either electronic books or paper books both from any one book publisher web store. So, electronic network platform may be one kind of good writing channel to help human authors to create income and it can also help authors to bring new creative mind and new topic fun content books to let readers to know and buy to read from electronic publisher network platform.

Why does human behavior may be one kind of new human network job to bring global economic advantages. ALthough, it may be free income or without inocme, but the person does the network behavior, his/her behavior may be bring advantages to influence many other people's health. For this case, when a worker in a coffee shop in an airport gets a vaccination aganinst the flu, it does not only helps him or her stay healthy, but also helps the many travellers who might otherwise have been inflected if that workers caught the flu. So, the externality , the result implies the vaccination of even a part of a community conveys benefits to the whole community. For example, governments pay special attention to the vaccinations of school children, teachers, health mothers, and the elderly, categories of people particularly susceptible not only to catching, but also to transmitting a disease.

It is not accidental that governments are heavily involved with vaccination . When there are externalities, free market, fail to persuade individual incentives with

society's
their the worker's decision of whether to get a vaccine ends up attracting whether other people get sick. The workers might not fully take all these other people's potential suffering into account when making her or his vaccination decision.

As Stanford University does many suggestions, understand this and tries to help them make the right decisions and so providers free flu vaccines for its staff and students.

Small pockets of unvaccinated individuals can allow a disease to gain a spread more widely well-being. For example, parent weighing the costs and benefits of a vaccine for their child is not always thinking of the consequences of that vaccination to other people. THese are markets in which subsidizing or regulating behavior can make everyone better off. Because the reason for requiring that a child be vaccinated before enrolling in school is not just to protect that child, because each child's vaccination affects others via potential contagions.

Robots take our jobs behavioral and economy influences
Robot job behavior brings economy influences

If one day robots can replace human to do simple, even complex jobs. They will bring what influences to our global societial economy.The popular economic refrain declares that the
global middle class is dying and robots will soon take our jobs, e.g. shopping center customer service jobs, library service jobs, cinema ticket sale jobs, restaurant kitchen cooker jobs,
even, bus drivers, taxi drivers etc. public transport driving jobs, accountant, doctors etc. professional jobs. Whether

it is beautiful or petty matter if our future societies have many human jobs can be replaced to do from robots. Businessman must may reduce to employ employees and reduce to pay salary or wage, when robots can be replaced to do their employees tasks. But, societies must bring unemployement rate rises , due to societies will have many people loss jobs when their employers choose to buy robots to serve their clients or do any office tasks or customer service or cleaning etc. tasks.

In micro economy view, employers may save money in long term, but in macro economy view, it will cause unemployment ratio rises , even crime rate rises when there are many people lose

jobs in societies. These models of doom, though, fail to account for the hundreds of businesses riding the waves of change in their industries when robots may be invented to replace human to do many simple , even complex tasks in our future societies.

WE may image that one small factory needs to manufacture fishes canes to sell to supermarket, the small , cheaper stuff and higher margin parts of the fishes manufacture industry. Before, this factory needs to employe many human factory workers need to help every fresh customer makeing the perfect fishing gear, designed for performance, durability, and cost in order to achieve to manufacture every fish cane in whole fished processing manufacturing stages. Every worker needs to spend about 15 to twenty minutes to finish every fish cane , till to delivery to any supermarket to sell. If this fish canes manufacturing factory can apply manufacturing robots to help them to finish any one working tasks , every robot can only spend five minutes to finish whole fresh fish cane manufacturing process. Thus, every robot can

help this factory save 10 to 15 minutes time to finsh every fish cane manufacturing process. IN fact, time is money, because when every robot can help this factory to reduce 10 to 15 minutes time to compare human worker. Then, this factory can finish about 20 fish canes in one hour if it can use robot to help it to manufacture fish canes. Otherwise, if this factory still use human workers to help it to manufacture fish canes, then it can finsh about 3 to 4 fish canes in one hour. SO, the manufacturing efficiency ensures that robots must help this fish manufacturing factory to raise fish canes number more than human workers. So, in robotic behavioral economy view, manufacturing robots must help this fish canes manufacturing factory to raise fish canes manufacturing number and deliver increasing number to supermarkets to prepare to sell every day. Robots can help this fish canes manufacturing factory bring manufacturing time saving, rising manufacturing efficiency, improving performance and reducing wages expenditure long time advantages in micro economy view. However, manufacturing robots can also bring disadvanages to society, e.g. increasing unemployment ratio, increasing crime rate,
this factory workers will lose jobs and income, they need earn social welfare from government and increasing government finance pressure in short time, even long time in macro economic view.

Stanford University graduate program in economics, Scott lecturer explained that "in demand and supply economic theory for robots supply and demand case, robots supply number increasing may influence human workers demand number decrease. It sometimes calls " the efficient frontier".
No specific human beings were mentioned in any of

economics classes. As robots supply and demand in market case, They (robots) may be purely theoretical " agents" who reached to the most reasonable sale prices in order to persuade any one businessman buyer to make manufacturing robot buying decision whether robots can help him / her to bring how much saving time , saving money, saving cost, improving performance, efficiency economic benefit before he/she plans to reduce workers number when he/she decides to apply robots to replace human workers in his/her factory or office or any service department, e.g. cinema ticket sale service, shopping center customer service, shopping center cleaning , supermarket customer service etc. service or sale tasks. When robots can replace human to do any one of these tasks in any organizations. So, robots may be human worker agents who reached to prices the way robots would react to a software command. There was nothing that explained why some people thrived and others did n't or why truly brilliant, hardworking people could fail when much lazier folks succeeded." Having been admitted to the Stanford University graduate program in economics, Scott lecturer hoped to get his answers there.

How robots influence our future social changing? Using the right technology can be a boon to your business in this economy. For internet example, it is easier than ever to find well-matched customers all around the world, to stay in contact with them, and to more quickly design the products they want. If you focus solely on being cutting -edge, though you risk letting the technology

take over what should be very robust relationships with your customers , employees, and colleagues. IN nowaddays society, technoligical advances and cutomation, personal relationships in business are more crucial than ever. I mean that robots can not replace human to serve clients to let them to feel more comfortable and passion more easily. For shoe shop case example, if the shoe shop apply one robot to serve its clients to replace human shoe salesperson to serve its shoe customers. Robots ensure that they can not persuade every shoe potential buyer to make shoe buying decision more easily when robots need to contact every shoe potential buyer. The reason is simple, because robots can not touch any one shoe buyer individual emotion very easier.

If the shoe buyer needs the robots to help him/her to choose any right shoe styles when he/she can not feel himself / herself can make the most right shoe style choice decision. The robots can not replace human shoe salesperson to make shoe style choice judgement more easily. They must need longer time to analyze whether which shoe style may be the most suitable to the shoe buyer. Otherwise, human shoe salesperson may attempt to make the most right shoe style choice decision to help any one shoe buyer to chooce the most right style shoe because he/she owns shoe style sale experience, shoe style knowledge, the most important reason is that they can feel every shoe customer individual emotion to touch whether he/she will feel comfortable or happy when they attempt to help every shoe customer to seek the most right shoe style in every shoe customer whole shoe searching processing. Othwerwise, serving robots are only one machine, they can not touch or feel every shoe customer individual emotion whether he/she feel comfortable or unhappy or happy when they need to contact them in whole shoe searching processing. Hence, I believe that some tasks robots can not repalce human staff to do very easily. Otherwise, robots may bring disadvanatges to let any one businessman to

loss his/her customers, due to robots can not touch every customer
emotion to compare human staff in service tasks more easily. Robots serving customer behaviors may cause money lose and customers number lose to the shop in micro economic view.

Intellectual human economic behaviors
What does intellectual human economic behaviors mean ? I believe that when we choose or decide to do intellectual behaviors, then our societies will be influenced to bring economic growth in consequence.I shall attempt to indicate pollution case to explain how and why eithet our intellectual or foolish behaviors may bring economic growth or recession in consequence as below:
On one hand, for air pollution social case aspect example, if we only consider to buy cars to drive for working aimr or holiday leisure aim. Then, our societies air will be polluted. Our health will be influenced to bad. Our car driving behaviors may cause global environment air pollution serously. In long tiem, global air pollution will bring our bodies health to be bad. Although, ourselves car driving behaviors may bring our driving travelling leisure enjoyment and comfortable feeling in short time, also we so not need to pay public transport fare often, but we need to compensate ourselves health economic intangible loss due to air pollution , when cars number increases, dirty air will cause ouselves health to become bad.
In the result, we will need to pay more medical expenditure when we are old age, due to ourselves bodies will become bad, due to we breathe global dirty air every day, due to ourselves cars pollute air in long time, e.g. 10 to 20 years, even 30 more without limited air pollution environment. So, driving cars behavior may be one kind of human foolish

behavior and our foolish behavior may bring ourselves future long time medical expenditure absolutely.

One the other hand, water pollution social aspect, if we often keep much rubblish to pollute sea, oil exploration porcessing pollute ocean , ships gas pollute ocaen, then fishes will eat polluted food and drive dirty water, due to global ocean is polluted.

In fact, because human only to conside how to buy boats to carry on leisure enjoyment activities, or catch cruises to travel on the sea. Also, oil manufacturers only consider researching anywhere to find new oil exploration places to manufacture oil product, when their oil exploration processes pollute ocarn . Consequently, global fishes drink polluted warer or eat polluted food. They will have poison. SO, human will have high chance to eat poison polluted fishes, due to fishes are poison or are polluted.

So, human is doing foolish activities, we only hope to find oil exploration places to pollute ocean or we only spend money to buy ticket to catch ships to travel anywhere in global ocean. All of these human foolish behaviors will bring pollution to global ocean. On consequently, we will need to compensate to eat polluted or dirty or poision fishes, ourselves bodies health will be bad. In long time, we need have high chance to pay medical expenditure when we are old. So, pollution case may be one good example to explain how and why human foolish behavior may influence ourselves future need to compensate serious medical loss.

All of these human foolish behavior will bring pollution to global ocean. On consequently, we will need to compensate to eat polluted or dirty or poison fished , ourselves bodies health will be bad. In long time, we will have high chance to pay medical expenditure, when we are old. So, pollution case may be one good example to explain how and why human ourselves intellectual or foolish behaviors may influence future long time economic loss or economic growth or recession in micro and micro economic view.

On another water pollution aspect hand, if we often keep rubbish to sea, oil exploration processing pollutes ocean and ships' gas pollute ocean, then fishes will eat polluted food and drink dirty water, due to fishes will eat polluted food and drink dirty sea water because the global ocean is polluted seriously.

In fact, because human only consider how to buy boats to carry on any leisure water activities, or catches cruises to travel on the sea. Also, oil manufacturers only consider any where to find oil exploratin places to manufacture oil products from ocean, when their pol exploration processes can plooute ocean. Consequently, global fishes drink polluted water or eat direty food. They will have poison. So, human will have high chance to eat poison fishes.

Otherwise, such as pollutin case, it can infuence inflation or deflation. Consequently, the reason indicates supply and demand theory. If air pollution is serious, then we will consider health issue, global cars demand number may be influenced to reduce, when global cars number demand will reduce, global car prices and supply number will need to change to fall down in order to attract or persuade global car consumers choose to make car purchase decision.

Hence, global car manufacture number and car price will be influenced to reduce, due to global air pollution issue. Consequently, deflation will occur because when the country citizen usually does not spend much extra saving money to buy car expensive goods. Money value will be low. Otherwise, if global cair pollution is not serious, human considers to buy cars to enjoy driving leisure lives.

So, global car demand is influenced to increase , also global car price will also influenced to increase.

Consequently, gobal human will choose to buy cars to drive. Due to we accept to spend extra saving to buy expensive car goods. Car sale price and supply may be influenced to rise up. Money value is influenced to reduce. Inflation may be influenced, due to global car consumers number increases, we would not have extra money to spend easily. Car expensive goods expenditure influences our spending habit to avoid to make car purchase decision more easily. So, human intellectual or foolish activities may bring inflation or deflation consequency in possible indirectly in macro economic view.

On conclusion, above pollution case explain that how and why human intellectual or foolish economic behaviors may bring inflation or deflation consequency as wll as economic growth or recession consequency as well as any goods demand and supply increasing or decreasing consequency. It implies that human behavior may have indirect relationship to influence any goods demand and supply number to either increase or decrease result as well as any goods price will be influenced to increase or decrease in micro and macro economic view.

The relationship between social change and human behavior

Why does economic changes may influence human individual behavioral change? I shall attempt to indicate shopping behavior and staying at home behavior to explain their case and effect relationsip as below:

Human behavior can be influenced by economic change or economic change can be influenced by human behavior? Why does recession may influence consumers reduce shopping desire? In social recession suitation, it is possible that many people lose jobs suddenly, due to businessmen lose many customers. They need to make decision to reduce employees number in order to continue to keep businesses. Consequently, many firms (organizations) their employees may lose jobs. When they have much time, due to lose jobs, they will feel to avoid to spend too much time and money to go to shopping often. Many losing jobs people, they will often stay at homes.

So, they will reduce time to go to shopping, then non essential products won't their preferable choice purchase products. Hence, recession will change many losing jobs people their shopping or consumption desires to avoid to buy non essential products often . Usually when economic boom, many people have jobs to do because consumers number must increase when many people have jobs to do. Then, many people can accept to spend money to buy non essential products often. Many people feel spend time to go to shopping can satisfy their purchase of any kinds of new products useful psychology or desire. So, recession is one good example to explain it can influence many people do not like often to leave homes to go to shopping easily. Many people like to stay at homes, becaue they feel worry about spending too much shopping time when they leave homes. Their staying home time is one good negative shopping behavior example. So, economic change may influence human individual behavior changes , they have direct cause and efect relationship in behavioral economic view.

May human behavior influence economic change? Is it possible that human behavior may bring the country social economic change in macro economic or micro behavioral economic view ? I shall indicate publishing industry example. Do you feel that if there are many students feel learning is very important when they read many books or many of students feel interesting to read or they have reading new books in habit, then it is possible that the country will have many students like to spend time to go to any book shops to choose the books, they feel that they can help they learn new knowledge. Then the country will increase students number, they often spend time to visit any one book shop every week. Their visiting book shops behavior which may become their habits. So, the country will increase students number, they often spend time to visit book shops. Also, it implies that visiting book shops behaviors may be their behavioral habits.

So, when the country has many students often spend time to visit book shops , their visiting book shops behaviors may help any one book shop to raise books sale chance. So, the country's student individual often visiting book shop behaviors, their habitual visiting book shops behaviors must may assist help any one book shop to increase books sale number absolutely.

Consequently, any one book shop , its books sale bumber must be influenced to increase to increase because the country will have many students like or feel need visit book shops habit in order to choose any suitable books to buy to read at home in order to raise themselves learning effort. When the country has many bok shops often have many students visit their book shops, then their books sale number may be influenced to increase. It explain why student individual visiting book shop behavior may help any one book shop sale number increases also.

How human productive behavior may influence economic development

May any country which citizen behavior assist themselves country development? It is one cause and effect economic question. I mean that if the country itself citicen can not concentrate mind or energy to choose to do one kind of industry in order to let themselves country can bring the most benefit, then whether the counry itself economy can bring the most serious economic benefit. I shall attempt to indicate these countries themselves indistry choice to explain whether these countries themselves citizen productive behavior may help themselves countries to achieve the largest economic benefits. I shall indicate as below:

New Zealand farmer individual wine productive behavior

For New Zealand country example, this country concerns itself effort is foucs on farming agricultural aspect. So, this country has many farmers concentrate on farming agricultural aspect. May New Zealanders choose to spend time to produce different kinds of wines, e.g. wine or red grape wine is for the people are eating meat, or they are eating dinner.

When these New Zealanders their behaviors choose to do farming or agriculture to grow and produce different kinds of taste of white or red grape wine drinking products job. Themselves grape agriculture behavior will influence these New Zealanders themselves, they can learn how to improve different kinds of grape wine drinking products in order to achieve every kinds of white or read grape wines taste improving aim during their white or red grape producing process.

Why can New Zealander every individual white or read grape wine producers improve their white or read grape wine taste more easily? In behavioral economic view, it can explain that why any one New Zealander white or read grape wine producer can be encouraged or excited or persuaded to concentrate nervous and energy and effort to learn how to improve their white or red grape wine products easily.

In fact, New Zealand is one agricultural food export country. It has good natural environment resource , e.g. land, seed to provide any one farmer to produce themselves any kinds of agricultrual food products, e.g. fruit, or wine food products. Because New Zealanders know themselves country has enough natural resource . So, in common, many New Zealanders choose to attempt to do farming agricultural jobs in order to export themselves any kinds of fruit or meat or wine products to overseas or sell to domestic in order to earn profit.

So, when these New Zealand farmers number has been increasing every year. This country farmers will feel themsleves competition between this New Zealand farmers themselves are serious due to they may feel New Zealanders choose to do agriculture businesses in order to export themselves different kinds of farming food to overseas or sell to local to earn profit.

Hence, when many New Zealand farmers feel that farmers number has been increasing every year. They will feel themselves competition is serious. They must need to spend much time and nervous and effort to research what method is the best how to produce the best taste of white or red grape wine products in order to let local or overseas wine buyers to choose to buy his/her producing white or read grpae products to drink.

Hence, in competition psychological view, may influence many New Zealand white or reaad wine producers had been beginning to change their learning behavior on researching what method is the best in order to produce the best quality of taste red or white wine products to sell in order to attract overseas or local white or read grape wine drinkers to choose to buy his/her wine products. Their behavior will focus on learning how to raising or improving white or read grape wine taste method more than only focus on producing a large number white or red grape wine products. They believe wine quality is more important to compare wine producing number. So, New Zealand wine producers themselves wine producers behaviors have been changing on concentrating on researching wine quality method aspect more then wine producing number aspect in behavioral economic view.

America high technological productive behavior
For America example, US is one high technological country, it owns many high technological knowledge talent inventors, e.g. computer science inventors. Hence, US must attract many diferent countries owning high technological computer inventors choose to go to US to develop their computer science profession career. Also, it seems that when many computer science inventors or professions choose to go to US to develop themselves computer science new career. In behavioral economic view, due to their leaving themselves countries choice, which may bring influence themselve country job behaviors need to be changed. They must need to adapt US new live. Because they will forgive their past computer science job. These computer science professionals need to spend time to adapt US new lives. They " past computer science job behaviors" will need to be changed to their new US any computer employer's new computer science job model.
Because their traditional computer science jobs needed to be forgot in their themselves countries. They will feel their old computer science job knowledge and behavior needed to change in order to let their US any one new of computer company employer feels satisfactory to accept their new working behavior in any one US computer organization.

So, on the other hand, many US computer company employer will feel that they must need time to accept any one new overseas computer science professions their working behaviors, their working attitude daily, because these foreign comouter sciencc professional, their past computer working behaviors and working attitude must be different to US domestic computer science professions.

In behavioral economic view, these overseas computer science professions, their working behaviors and attitude must be needed to change in order to adapt any one US new computer company itself domestic or local computer science professional stafs themselves daily working behaviors and attitude because these overseas and local computer science professionals must need to team work together.

In behavioral economic view, it is only one way that foreign computer science professionals must need to change themselves past country traditiona daily working behaviors and attitude in order to cooperate with these US local computer science professionals in teams more easily.

Consequently, if these foreign compute science professionals can change their past working behaviors and attitude to let any one US local computer science professional feels to cooperate with them easily in short time. Then, the US computer company itself whole computer professional teams themselves efficiencies will be influenced to raised or improved by the changing past working attitude and working behaviors of these foreign computer science professionals. So, in behavioral economic view, only if US any one computer company hopes itself computer teams themselves efficiency can be raised or improved when it decides to employ foreign computer science professionals and US domestic computer science professionals. They need to work in teams together. They must need to let these foreign computer science professionals to know how to change their working behaviors and attitude to let their domestic computer science professionals feel easy to work together. Then, the US computer company itself whole team efficiency must be rasied or improved easily in short time.

● China share market investing behavior

For China share market example, economic development depends on financial market. Because if many Chinese have interest to invest to carry on shares buying and selling activities in orde to learn how to earn shares interest and share profit when the China shareholder can make decision to sell himself/herself shares in the the high price, then he/she can earn money when he/she can sell the China company's shares in the high sale share price position.

If China has many Chinese like to spend time to carry on investing shares activities. Themselves shares buying and selling behaviors will influence China has many companies can increase fund from many Chinese shareholders in order to have enough money to expand or develop themselves businesses in China in long term.

Consequently, when China can have many Chinese like to attempt to carry on buying and selling shares investing behaviors in China share market. Themselves buying and selling shares behaviors can help many Chinese companies have effort to increase enough money or capital in order to continue to do their businesses in long term absolutely. So, it explains why when many Chinese become shareholders , they can assist China will have many companies continue to develop their businesses if many Chinese like to carry on shares buying and selling investing behaviors in long time in China financial investment market nowadays in behavioral economic view.

Why has any individual country have many people invest share behavior which can influence the country's macro consumption desire?

I shall apply shares market buying and selling investment behavior to explaiin why shares investment behavior which may impact the country's overal consumption desire as below:

In behavioral economic view, I assume that when the coutry has many people have interest to attempt to carry on shares buying and selling investment behavior, then their frequent shares buying and selling behaviors which may bring negactive consumption desire or shopping desire of these shares investors their consumer behavior.

The reason is simple, when the country has many share buyers number suddenly been increasing rapidly. Consequently, these large group share investors must need to spend much time to research any kinds of company shares variations, whether when their share prices will rise up of fall down in order to achieve buying the company's shares in the lowest price and selling the company's shares in the highest price level in order to earn profit.

Basic on this reason, they must need to spend much extra time to research share prices changing behavior every day, e.g. one working person will wait to leave his/her job, after he/she can spend time to gather data to research the day's share price changing behavior after dinner. So, the working person's right time may be his/her share price market research behavior. Before he/she may spend his/her night time to go to shopping after dinner, but nowadays, he/she will fogive to do his/her shopping behavior before dinner or after dinner at hight sometime. He/she will make decision to spend much night time to turn on computer to click on share market website to research his/her share purchase choice to investigate whether his/her share price whether it rises up or falls down at the moment in order to make his/her share buying or selling decision at ever night time.

I mean the when the country has many people are share investors, their shares investment behavioral spenging time which will influence many shops lose customers at might often because the country will have many people feel need to spend night time to turn on computer or watch television to investigate share price variation. So, the country will have many people / share investors choose to stay at home in order to carry on share price variation investigation behavior, they need to listen share market update news from radios or watch the share market update news from computer or TV at home every night. Consequenly, they must reduce times to leave themselves homes at night. So, their shopping behavior also will be reduced. Because these share investors feel need to spend time to investigate share price variation news at homes which can bring economic benefits (high opportunity benefits) when they choose to forgive to leave homes to go to shopping times (opportunity cost) every night.

On conclusion, it seems that when the country has many people are share investors, then their share price investigating behavior may bring negative shopping emotion at night. Consequently, the country's any one shop may lose many customers from this share investor consumer group in behavioral economic view. Hence, when the country's share investors number had been increasing rapidly, it will influence any shops lose many customers from this share investing customer group at night frequently in short time, even long time in behavioral economic view, because their shopping desires or shopping emotion will be brought negative feeling when they make decisions to spend much time to listen radios or watch TV or computers share price update nes at night. Hence, share market will bring negative impact to influence consumer shopping desire or negative shopping emotion in behavioral economic view.

Can technology influence human shopping behavioral change?

Nowadays, technological development has reached mature stage, whether technological mature stage may bring positive or negative shopping emotion influence to global consumers. I shall aplly internet inventin or ecommerce shopping channel tool to explain whether internet technology can bring postive or negative influence to global consumer behavior in behavioral economic view.

Internet is a good technological tool, it brings e-commerce business chance. In fact, commonly, global has have many businessmen choose to use internet channel to carry on their products transactions between global online-buyers and their electronic websites. So, global many shoppers had begun to feel online shopping is more convenient to compare visiting shops shopping. Their shopping behaviors have been changed from internet technological tool. Global has many shoppers choose to buy any products from any overseas or local businessmen their web stores. They only need to spend time to find any businessmen their webstores to choose the most suitable products to pay visa to buy from their webstores. at homes. So, in general, global had have may shoppers had changed their shopping behaviors from visiting shops to visiting webstores at homes often.

So, it seems that internet technological tool had influenced global many shops disappear, but internet webstores will be replaced their actual shops on streets. Some of businessmen either they choose webstores to replace shops or choose websotes and shops both or still keep shops only. Hence, internet tool influences global businessmen have three kinds of products sale channels to let globa local and overseas consumers to choose how to buy their products.

However, in fact, many of global shoppers, youngers and olders had begun to accept to buy any products from webstores. They feel to spend time to leave homes to visit shops , their shopping behaviors will be wasted time to not essential part to their daily lives. Hence, since internet technological invention, it had changed many consumers their traditional visiting shops shopping habit to change to buying products from webstores channel.

However, on the one hand, internet creates webstores ecommerce shopping channel to let global many consumers do not need to leave homes to go to shopping. It brings negative visiting shops shopping emotion to global general consumers nowadays. But on the other hand, it also brings positive visiting internet webstores shopping emotion to global general consumer nowadays. So, it seems that global many consumers feel that they often do not need to spend much time to go out shopping. Many global consumers feel convenient and enjoy to choose any products to buy from different internet webstores, when the online buyer chooses the most suitable product, he she only needs to pay visa card to buy the product from the online seller's webstore conveniently at home.

Hence, online shopping can bring economic benefit to online buyers, e.g. avoiding walking time or spending transport fare to visit the shop to go to shopping, shortening or reducing shopping time to do another important matter.

On conclusion, global many consumers began feel online shopping can bring more economic benefits on shortening shopping time, avoiding transport fare spending aspect. So, online shopping will be popular shopping behavior for future long time. It may encourage global many shoppers can make rapid shopping decision in short time in order to carry on any products buying transaction to global any one online shopper in short time easily in behavioral economic view. So, global many businessmen had begun to build themselves one attraction webstore in order to persuade different countries consumers to choose to click themselves webstores from internet channel to buy any kinds of products in short time easily.

So, internet technology had changed consumers traditional shopping behaviors to build positive online shopping emotion as well as raise online sellers' any products sale chance easily in behavioral economic view.

Why and how human behavior may influence the country's economic growth or recession?

When one country has many people choose to do the same matter for one period, whether their behavior may influence the country's pvera; economic growth or recession . I shall attempt to indicate cases toexplain their relationship as below:

For flowing rubblish behavioral case example, do you feel that when the country has many people often flow rubblish on the streets, instead of their flowing rubblish behavior may bring streets dirty? But, their flowing rubblish behavior may explain that this country has people may have enough money to buy food to ear, or enough cloths to wear, enough bottles of water to drink, even they may have enough money to buy new television, radio, refrigeraters , washing machines, desktops or laptops electronic home products from old to new to use in order to satisfy their living needs. So, when they flow old electronic home products, their flowing old home electronic products behaviors may seem that they have enough money to buy other new home electronic products to replace old home electronic products to use at homes.

However, it seems thaat this country ought have many people have jobs to do. So, many of them, they can easy to make purchase decison to flow any old home electronic products and buy any new home electronic products to use . Because this country has many people have jobs to do. So, they can often not use old home electonic products to become rubblishs to flow on streets after they had bought any kinds of new home electronic homes.

In fact, it also implies that this country's economy grows rapidly. So, many businesses can glow up rapdly. When they expanded their businesses, they must need to increase employees number in order to let they help themselves to raise productivity or serve their clients absolutely. So, when the country has many businesses can grow up, it seems that its economy must be better or it is improved to compare past. Due to many different kinds of home electronic products had been often bought to use by this country people in this period. So, this country's any streets can be observed that expensive electronic home products were flowed on streets anywhere. then, this country will have many electronic home products sellers can sell their home electronic products very easily. When this country has many people can find any kinds of jobs to do easily. So, due to unemploymen rate had been decreasing.

In behavioral economic view, as this many electronic home

products rubblish country case, we can observe this country may have many people have jobs to do. So, consumption number has been increased long time. So, cheap food, or expensive home electronic products may be rubblish on any streets. This country's people , their flowing rubblish behaviors may be explained that many of people have enough jobs to do, so they have ability to buy any good taste food to eat or buy any kinds of expensive electronic home products to use. So, this country's economy may be improved for this long period. So, in behavioral economic view, when this country can have many electronic home products rubblishs are flowed on anywherer in streets frequently. It seems that this country will have many people have jobs to do, so it causes they often change old home electronic products or replaced them easily, when they have enough income to spend to buy any kinds of new home electronic products to use at homes easily. Moreover, their flowing old electronic home products behaviors also indicate that this country has many people their salaries may be increased in possible from their emplyers. When this country can have many different kinds of home electornic products are sold. It means that this country's electronic home products needs or demand had been increasing, due to many people have jobs to do and income increases to excite their living of needs also improve. Consequently, this country may seem have better economic improvement. We can observe from this country's electronic home products rubblish increasing income in theis period.

On conclusion, this country ought experience economic growth at this period. So, " flowing expensive electronic home rubblish increasing number " may seem that this country's economic growth is rapidly in this period, due to many people have jobs to do as well as salaries increase in this period.